CW00766262

BEYOND WORDS

A YEAR WITH KENNETH COOK

BEYOND WORDS

A YEAR WITH KENNETH COOK

JACQUELINE KENT

UQP

First published 2019 by University of Queensland Press
PO Box 6042, St Lucia, Queensland 4067 Australia

www.uqp.com.au
uqp@uqp.uq.edu.au

Cover design by Sandy Cull, gogoGingko
Author photo by Kiren Photography
Typeset in 12.5/16 pt Perpetua MT by Post Pre-press Group, Brisbane
Printed in China by 1010 Printing Asia Limited

Australia Council for the Arts

The University of Queensland Press is assisted by the Australian Government through the Australia Council, its arts funding and advisory body.

ISBN 978 0 7022 6039 1 (hbk)
ISBN 978 0 7022 6207 4 (ePDF)
ISBN 978 0 7022 6208 1 (ePub)
ISBN 978 0 7022 6209 8 (Kindle)

A catalogue record for this book is available from the National Library of Australia.

University of Queensland Press uses papers that are natural, renewable and recyclable products made from wood grown in sustainable forests. The logging and manufacturing processes conform to the environmental regulations of the country of origin.

CONTENTS

For everyone who was there,
and for Sophie

INTRODUCTION

On the shelf above my desk is a battered exercise book, the kind used by generations of Australian primary school children – one that, in defiance of calculators, has tables of cubic tonnes and hectares and other measurements marching across the back cover. On the front cover is a small panel with these words printed carefully by hand: *Name:* Kenneth Bernard Cook *School:* Fort Street Boys' High *Age:* 56 and ¾.

That exercise book, one of the few tangible legacies of my brief marriage, is my portal into the past. Whenever I look at it I see a tall man with curly salt-and-pepper hair and a piratical beard hunched over a too-small desk, squinting through smeared glasses held together with sticky tape as words flowed smoothly from the nib of his fountain pen onto the page. A glass of Victoria Bitter or whisky and a cigarette always stood ready whenever inspiration failed, which it rarely did, though the glass was always emptied. If he couldn't think of a word for a minute or two he would scribble. He often drew long, strange animals with droopy tails, whiskers and lolling tongues, and crosses for eyes. Once I asked him why he kept drawing pictures of rats. He explained rather huffily that they were not rats but ferrets, and that he just liked drawing them, that was all. But there were often times when numbers, not words, flowed from his fluent pen. Several pages of that exercise book display columns of figures and percentages, all related to money, income and expenditure. In the time we were together, and thereafter, these calculations had a greater influence on our shared life than any words he wrote.

The fact that Ken and I got together at all still surprises me. Though we were bonded by our love of books and writing, for me words were instruments of explanation, clarity and concision, both in my own writing and in my work as an editor. Ken on the other hand was first and foremost a storyteller, a man who often used words for dramatic effect, who gambled on always being able to sell the work he produced, a man who assumed that every business enterprise of his would be successful. He also believed that money, however obtained, existed to be spent; being financially conservative to the point of caution, I hadn't had a lot of practice in taking risks.

Ken had one great stroke of luck at the beginning of his literary career, of course, twenty-five years before we met. He was only in his early thirties when he published *Wake in Fright*, the novel on which his reputation still largely rests. The novel, published in 1961 and written out of an understanding of human frailty, a dislike of the cherished Aussie myth of mateship and a deep sense of pessimism, opened a lot of doors for Ken – though I don't think he really knew, as writers often don't, how he managed to make this particular novel resonate so powerfully.

It seemed to me, and still does, that for every quality he possessed he embodied its opposite. He was cool-headed, passionate, sensible, wrong-headed, tough and sentimental, an intensely urban man who yearned to lose himself in the world outside Australia's cities, a social snob who was happy to be a friend to anyone, a politically conservative anarchist, a truthful and honest man who would spin any yarn he thought he could get away with, a lunatic optimist with a strong sense of doom, and – like many Australians of Irish background – a hard-headed realist with an imaginative, even mystical, streak a mile wide. He could turn an argument on a sixpence, begin defending a stance he had just spent half an hour attacking. I never knew quite what I was getting, never quite came to the end of him. We had times of rich domestic tranquillity, upsets that were enraging at times, and I was never, ever bored. Just that last, I have always believed, is worth a great deal.

I'd never met anyone like Ken Cook, and I haven't since. When I look back and consider the relatively flat plain of my life before his volcanic eruption into it, I still cannot quite believe the time we spent together. Not because it was always wonderful – it wasn't. Like many extreme events, human as well as geological, our association had sharp and potentially dangerous edges, visible from many sides. This is why – though it's not the only reason – I am charting its topography in these pages.

PART 1

BECAUSE HE WAS HE, BECAUSE I WAS I

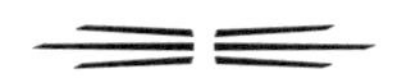

If you press me to say why I loved him,
I can say no more than because he was he,
because I was I.
MICHEL DE MONTAIGNE

A MEETING OF MINDS

It was July 1985 and I had been unexpectedly invited to a dinner party. People had them in those days. The hostess, whom I shall call Clare, was a woman I knew professionally rather than a friend: I had never thought we were close enough for me to be invited to her house. Certainly we both edited books for a living, but I wasn't sure what else we had in common. Small, neat and very English, Clare had worked in London publishing for many years – a world, we Australian book editors assumed, of calm and tradition, where family background was all-important and where most of the men who ruled the industry, and their employees, came from public schools and had private incomes. My own experience in London, brief though it had been, bore this out. On my first day as an editorial assistant to a London publisher about ten years before, I had seen the sales manager descending the staircase in striped trousers, cutaway coat and top hat on his way to Ascot.

We Australian editors, working mostly for the American- and British-based publishers who had dominated the local scene since the 1970s, snickered happily at the thought of any sales manager we had ever met doing such a thing. However, we did have one important thing in common with our UK counterparts: we were badly paid. Being a fairly bolshie lot, though, we were trying to do something about it. We asked no favours but claimed our right to a fair deal and, to Clare's fastidious horror, we had launched a lobbying campaign for more money and better conditions. Though this had been partially successful, Clare had made known very gently – as only the English can – that confronting one's bosses about money was unnecessary and even rather vulgar. Surely it was better to work behind the scenes, to persuade gradually. We scorned such an oblique way of doing things, and made this clear to her – as only Australians can.

Clare and I had never argued about this directly, but we were both aware that we were not exactly soulmates. So I thought it was generous of her to ask me to dinner, though the invitation still puzzled me slightly. The meal would be casual, she explained, nothing flash. The other guests were an Australian independent publisher and a bookshop owner and their wives, not all of whom

I knew. Clare asked me to bring the man I was seeing at the time, a former journalist who had worked for *Reader's Digest*, as did Clare herself. Maybe she wanted to talk to him, I thought. He was a very pleasant and affable man a fair bit older than I, and someone who, I knew, could be relied upon to ensure the conversation did not steer into any awkward corners.

Clare added that she was also inviting her fiancé. She gave the word a wry Jane Austenish twist, as if she'd said 'affianced' or 'betrothed'. I already knew that the man in question was not Mr Darcy. Indeed, when the word of this engagement had got out in publishing circles, the reaction had been a mixture of laughter and incredulity. The fastidious, patrician Clare intended to marry *Kenneth Cook*? Really? I had never met Kenneth Cook, but many publishing people had; he had been around since at least the 1960s and had written about a dozen novels, the best known of which was *Wake in Fright*, made into a classic film some years before. People spoke with awe about the amount of alcohol he got through without any apparent effect, how quickly and professionally he could turn out words, and I had been told that his family setup was rather odd. But nobody I knew went into detail about any of these things, and my impression was that he held himself a little aloof from literary circles.

People, whether they knew him or not, tended to

declare that Kenneth Cook was *larger than life*. They would say this in a slightly self-congratulatory way, as if this hackneyed expression was the best and only way to describe him. (It's a phrase almost always applied to men, by the way: maybe the thought is that women can generally be cut down to size.) This had put me off the idea of him for a start. A professional booze artist with a non-standard family? How was this *larger than life*, and how *large* is life anyway? But I did know that calling someone *larger than life* is rarely a compliment, like describing someone as *a character* – another phrase I had heard applied to Kenneth Cook. For me both these expressions conjured up a pompous, boring male – indeed, the kind of person skewered by Emily Dickinson as a 'somebody' like a bullfrog croaking his name *the livelong June – / To an admiring Bog*.

But I wasn't entirely sure that Kenneth Cook was this kind of person. For one thing, I couldn't imagine Clare, calm and punctilious as she was, putting up with a bullfrog. But more importantly, I had read *Wake in Fright* and seen the film: the truth and bleakness of that particular story, sparsely written and with flashes of sardonic humour, had stayed with me. And so my mental picture of the novel's author was not of a loud bully but of a tall, spare grasshopper of a man with a grim cast of mind and a bitten-back sense of humour. On balance, then, I thought the dinner party was likely to be interesting and I looked forward to it.

Clare's house was in Stanmore, a part of Sydney I have always liked. It had once been a rather grand suburb of large Victorian houses with black and white marble paths sweeping up to column-flanked porches, of bay windows and parquet floors and ballrooms and shady verandahs. But after two wars and a depression, not to mention the frenzy of demolition unleashed by the Sydney City Council during the 1960s, many of those houses had disappeared or were in varying stages of disrepair. More recently, in some parts of the suburb it seemed possible to touch the bellies of the shrieking 747s on their way to the airport. So now Stanmore's attraction was not the prosperity of its residents but its proximity to the University of Sydney. The elegant bay windows displayed bright bedspreads in Indian cotton as curtains, and solid wooden front doors were plastered with PEACE and NO NUKES stickers. I always liked the untidiness, the raffishness of Stanmore, and I never went there without wishing I was a student again, a proper, serious one with books to read and essays to write. But Stanmore's days as a student suburb were already numbered. Gentrification was once more on its way, with the tide of Tuscan apricot or forest green paint beginning to lap at its streets.

Clare's house on the edge of the suburb was small,

pleasant and unfussy, like Clare herself. Her front room was, as I had expected, full of books, mostly on home decoration and English history, with a few large volumes on art. Not much fiction – perhaps she kept that somewhere else. But I did notice a hardback copy of *Poor Fellow My Country* by Xavier Herbert, winner of the Miles Franklin Award a decade previously and well known as the longest novel ever published in Australia. Like Stephen Hawking's *A Brief History of Time* years later, *Poor Fellow* was famous for being owned but not read. If Clare had actually read it, she was ahead of me.

My date and I were the last to arrive. In the sitting room Clare introduced us to the other guests. I was conscious of being the youngest in the group; Clare somehow managed to suggest that I had left my King Gee overalls and SISTERHOOD IS POWERFUL placards at the front door. The other guests were from the business side of publishing rather than the literary side, and the conversation soon settled to discussions about sales figures, sizes of local print runs, amounts paid for the rights of overseas books, how much business people expected to do at the Frankfurt Book Fair that year. I started to wish someone would throw a stone into this conversational pond, but nobody seemed interested in starting ripples. Not being this kind of provocateur myself I sat sipping my white wine, feeling I had very little to contribute.

Holding a glass and saying so little meant I had an excellent opportunity to observe Kenneth Cook, who was seated on the other side of the room and who, like me, was mostly silent. The first thing I noticed was how inaccurate my preconceptions had been. Here was no lean, sardonic bushman; no loud-voiced dullard either. He had curly hair, a beard, shaggy dark eyebrows, green eyes and very even white teeth. A writer from Central Casting, 1960s bohemian division, I decided. He was wearing grey trousers and a meek maroon jumper, but should have been in corduroy trousers and a tweed jacket with leather elbow patches. I mentally composed an 'about the author' blurb: *Kenneth Cook enjoys red wine and jazz, especially* Kind of Blue *by Miles Davis. A prolific novelist, he builds and sails wooden yachts in his spare time …*

But my first impression, again, was immediately contradicted. Though he was about six feet tall and solidly built he did not look particularly powerful, having narrow shoulders and long, thin arms and legs. Not, I guessed, a man who spent time outdoors building things. He looked on edge, taking frequent sips from his glass of red wine and puffing avidly on his cigarette. Nobody else in the room was smoking, and I knew Clare disliked it, but guessed that she had relaxed her house rules for him. Altogether he gave an impression of suppressed energy, of contained restlessness. Indeed, there were a few minutes – while the others were talking about the Frankfurt Book Fair – when I wondered whether boredom would overcome politeness and he would actually get up and leave.

We moved to the table and Clare served dinner. I noticed that Kenneth did not offer to help and Clare did not ask him to pour the wine or bring any food from the kitchen, though other guests did. I marked Ken Cook down for that, but as the meal progressed his lack of any domestic or co-hosting involvement began to intrigue me. Though I had no particular expectations about how couples of mature years should behave in public – and certainly did not want to witness the shared knowing smiles, touches of hands, glances and private jokes that can be so tedious for outsiders – I saw nothing that indicated Clare and Kenneth Cook meant much more to each other than dinner guest and hostess. For two people who presumably intended to marry, their apparent distance from each other was mystifying.

Over the chicken casserole and green salad, the bookseller asked Ken politely what he was writing. Thinking this might be the cue for a bit of *larger than life* behaviour, I braced myself for the sort of self-important explanation of My Work I had seen in other writers of his vintage. But no. He said diffidently that he was working on a couple of projects, nothing very big. It was clear that he was not about to say any more, and the conversation drifted back to sales figures and print numbers, and then to Reader's Digest Books.

At the time Reader's Digest were putting large amounts of money into original, lavishly illustrated volumes about Australian history, flora and fauna, and actively looking for Australian novels for their Condensed Books series. Like other Australian editors at the time I was somewhat snobbish about Reader's Digest Condensed Books. We thought they represented yet another example of aggressive US cultural hegemony at work, not least because Digest's editorial policy was often to rewrite, shorten and homogenise Australian books. As far as we could see, this meant getting rid of any local colour and striking down adjectives and adverbs without mercy. What about the writer's individual voice? we asked self-righteously. Had Australian novelists laboured for years to have their evocative and tender prose obliterated and replaced by the literary equivalent of Spakfilla? We were aware, of course, that many local writers we knew disagreed with our position: RD paid very well, and outrage about stylistic alterations came a long way behind taking the money and running. But in our eyes that did not excuse what these American imperialists were doing.

I learned that Kenneth Cook's novel *Tuna*, about an impoverished South Australian fisherman and his attempts to land the biggest fish of his life, had been published by Condensed Books to some acclaim. I had been drinking white wine for a while by now, and was becoming irritated by the enormous respect that publication by Reader's Digest seemed to attract from the other guests. It was, then, with perhaps a small touch of aggression that I asked Kenneth, 'So what did the Digest call your novel when they'd finished with it? *Sardine*?'

There was a small silence. My dinner partner shot me a sideways glance. Nobody laughed – except Kenneth. 'Nope,' he told me. 'They did it just as it was.'

'That's very rare,' added my partner quickly; I could see that he wanted to smooth things over.

'Right,' I said. 'Must be a good story.'

'Oh, it is,' Kenneth assured me, his eyes twinkling. 'I'm sure you'll enjoy it. I'll get you a copy.' The conversation moved on, but he kept glancing at me speculatively.

One evening a couple of weeks later I was at home in my apartment when my phone rang. 'This is Kenneth Cook,' said a deep, cultivated voice. 'I'm in the pub just around the corner from your place. Come and have a drink with me.'

No *Hello*, *how are you* or *are you free* . . . And how the hell did he get my number, anyway? Let alone know where I lived?

When I asked him, he chuckled. 'I have my methods,' he said. 'Well, what about it?'

'Sorry,' I said. 'I'm on a deadline.' I wasn't, but I had been caught by surprise, and I wanted to think about this.

My reply did not faze him in the least, and he said he would call again. A few days later he did, and I said no, this time with some indignation: who did this bloke think he was, asking me out when he was practically married to someone else – and to a colleague at whose house I had met him?

He rang yet again, and again, and I kept saying no. 'Well, when can you come out with me then?' he asked tersely. 'Tomorrow? Tuesday, Thursday week? Next Pancake Day ... oh no, you'll probably have to wash your hair that evening ...' He didn't seem seriously annoyed at any time, and neither was I. I could certainly have told him to get lost and made that stick, but for some reason I didn't want to. There was no animosity in our conversations, which on the whole felt like a kind of friendly game, perhaps a circling around each other. This was probably why I felt a stab of regret when he stopped ringing me, though I knew how completely illogical this was.

A couple of months later I heard that he and Clare

were no longer engaged; nobody, including me, thought that this was the most surprising news they had ever heard. Clare had called a halt to the arrangement because she said she *couldn't stand living on the edge.* I wondered about her choice of words, but life grew busy and I dismissed it from my mind.

And then towards the end of the year I opened a copy of *The National Times* to see a photograph of Kenneth Cook with a large and alarming bandage round his head. It came with a longish article, which he had written, describing his operation to replace an artery in his head to prevent a stroke. I was really shocked to discover he had been so ill. But the tone of the piece was airy, almost light-hearted: there were no reflections about mortality, but a certain triumphalism, a celebration of having survived, cheated death. The article gave few family details, just mentioning that he was separated from his wife and had four adult children (the inability to wrestle with his 'strapping sons' was a cause of regret, it seemed).

For a moment I wished I had kept in touch, could make an effort to contact him and say how sorry I was that this had happened. However, I told myself I really didn't want to encourage him to call me again. So I left it, and gradually forgot about him.

Looking back, I can see how settled my life was then, and I told myself I had arranged things much the way I wanted them. Following a pattern established for more than ten years I lived in a small apartment, worked alone and supported myself. Kipling's cat who walked by herself – that was me, or at least I liked to think so.

My literary career – if that's what it was – seems now to be a matter of impulse, of opportunity, with very little planning. Having started off as a journalist on a TV magazine, I had spent a few years as a children's radio producer with the ABC in Sydney before tossing it in to work overseas. This was the time when living in London was a glamorous thing to do, at least to people who had never tried it. Existing on money from temporary secretarial jobs – the great dream of breaking into the BBC remained exactly that – I moved through a succession of cabbage-smelling bedsits, saving as much as I could to go to the theatre and the opera and museums and to buy books. I was also trying to write, and amassing the Wallace Collection of rejection letters from newspapers and magazines and book publishers. It was all hard work, but certainly not depressing: my naïve optimism, knowing I had prospects and possibilities, however nebulous, kept me afloat. Trudging home from the Tube through the freezing darkness of a winter afternoon and living on noodles in a damp room are fine if you can transform what you see around you into Material.

I certainly met enough characters to put into the novel I was going to write someday. One of my favourites was the independent publisher Peter Owen. His obituary in *The Guardian* a few years ago paid due tribute to his achievements in bringing European writers to the attention of English readers, but that is not what I remember about him. He was a short and erratic man, even shambolic, with a harsh voice and mad Einstein grey hair, a wearer of expensive suits with trousers trailing on the floor and important buttons missing. But his office in Holland Park laid claim to some grandeur. Indeed, it had been Peter Owen's sales manager whom I beheld in all his Ascot-bound glory.

I learned that Owen's authors included Anaïs Nin,

Hermann Hesse and – when she and Owen were on speaking terms, which wasn't often when I was there – Doris Lessing. These were just names to me; I never met any of them, nor had I read their work (I caught up some years later). I spent most of my time in the tiny back room of that Georgian mansion filing and typing letters, arguing with Peter about getting the ancient and decrepit photocopier repaired one more time ('Can't you just type out the contract again?') and trying to throw away used office stationery, not with much success. I would come into work in the morning to find him glowering over the wastepaper basket. 'Look at this!' he would caw at me, holding aloft a sheet of black carbon paper. 'Why did you throw this away?' When I pointed out that it was peppered with tiny holes and therefore useless as a copying device, he would snort, 'There's at least another week left in this!' I took to smuggling the used carbon paper out of the office and getting rid of it in council street bins.

However, Peter Owen proved to be useful for more than just Material. When I returned to Australia I was able to parlay my experience with him into a job as an editorial assistant at Reeds, a New Zealand-based publisher of natural history and educational books. I couldn't believe my luck: I was being paid roughly twice what I had been earning in London, and I had embarked on a career in publishing. And so I traded an office in a London terrace with antique furniture and Anatolian rugs for one in a warehouse the size of an aircraft hangar on the northern bush fringes of Sydney. Crouched behind bookcase partitions, the staff froze in winter and sweltered throughout the fierce bushfire-smoky summer. Between November and March the only cool spot in the place was the air-conditioned room in which dwelt the God of the Sales Department, the enormous state-of-the-art computer.

In the late 1970s and early 1980s, local publishing was expanding. Though it was dominated by British and American companies, at least they were publishing books by Australian writers for Australian readers. There were more books, more writers, more stories, and it was exciting to be part of all that, however small my role was. After a while I left Reeds for another publisher – Cassell Australia, like so many other medium-sized publishers later swallowed up by a conglomerate – and then became a freelance editor, working on a project-by-project basis for several publishing houses.

I enjoyed being able to concentrate on the work at hand without factoring in office politics, personalities and meetings. Besides, the range of manuscripts I worked on was vast, ranging from novels to illustrated children's books and tomes about natural history. I even worked on something called *Modern Electrical Wiring*, a job that mostly involved making sure diagrams were in the right place, though I never really knew what they were for. Generally, the work suited me very well. On good days – and there were many – helping authors to write better books felt like an honourable craft, an honest and useful thing to do. In those days, before it was possible for a book to go all the way from author to printer as a one-dimensional array of bytes somewhere in the ether, manuscripts were living things. Those piles of paper with pencil markings like bird tracks, crossings-out, paragraphs chopped up and sticky-taped to pages and sentences selectively obliterated in a blizzard of Tipp-Ex could seem as huge, creative and messy as the process of thought itself.

In 1984 I moved into an apartment in North Sydney that I loved. I had discovered it by sheer chance: I had been walking down a street of bland suburban bungalows when I came upon an apartment house – it looked too small to be a block of flats – called Bellarion Court. It had white stucco walls and a front door of toffee-coloured wood guarded by two green-painted pillars twisted like pieces of barley sugar. A vaguely heraldic stained-glass window above the entrance cast shadows of ruby and gold. Bellarion Court combined *Ivanhoe*, *Sunset Boulevard* and *Hansel and Gretel*, and I knew immediately that I had to live there.

The local newsagent told me that the house had

been built during the Depression by a father and his two sons from the central west of New South Wales; they had intended it as a boarding house and after the war converted it into apartments for rent. The last remaining member of the trio, a tall, silver-haired man in his seventies who could have been the butler in *Sunset Boulevard* except for his slow Aussie drawl, still lived in the building. He personally vetted all tenants and had no truck with leases, children or pets. He told me that no apartments were available at the moment, but he would let me know when something came up.

When I asked why he had named the place Bellarion Court, he told me he didn't know, that the family had just liked the name. But I discovered that Bellarion the Fortunate was the swordsman hero of a novel by Rafael Sabatini, author of *Captain Blood* and other swashbuckling historical novels widely read during the 1920s and 1930s; he and his father might have adopted it. I was pleased that the building had literary associations and liked the thought that this building, like its heroic namesake, was standing ready to fend off bad men, in this case evil property developers.

It took three months before I was able to move into Bellarion Court. Number 7 was on the bottom level of the building, down two steep flights of stairs and along a narrow cream-painted passage. Light off the harbour made watery lines on the ceiling. It was like walking down the corridor of a passenger liner in the 1930s.

The flat, which was part furnished, consisted of a living room, kitchen, small alcove bedroom and a tiny bathroom. To the coldly appraising eye it was on the shabby side: the wallpaper in the living room was lumpy, the grey carpet was frayed, the wooden sash windows screeched in protest whenever they were opened. The kitchen was long and narrow, with a round table and chairs at one end and a sink at the other. The gas stove, an Early Kooka with a kookaburra emblazoned on the door, reminded me of the kitchen in my grandmother's house when I was a child. I appreciated its sentimental value but it wasn't great for cooking: roasting a leg of lamb could easily take half a day. I sometimes thought that if Sylvia Plath had had that oven, she would probably still be alive. But I loved Number 7 from the moment I walked in. Light danced through all the rooms: I could gaze down through a scrim of trees and morning glory on the sparkling waters of Lavender Bay. From the kitchen table, my books and papers spread out as I edited some manuscript or other, I would watch commuters picking their way to the ferry across the disused railway tracks that curved around one side of the bay. It was like looking into a Tom Roberts painting.

More than anything else, what I enjoyed about Number 7 was its quiet and privacy: as soon as I shut the door behind me I was in my little cave, all by myself. I enjoyed the solitude, I felt literary and self-sufficient – a freewheeling writerly spirit from an earlier epoch, perhaps Stevie Smith or Winifred Holtby, frowning below her 1930s fringe while a novel formed itself purposefully under her hand. By this time I had published one book of non-fiction, a history of Australian radio based on interviews with many of those who had worked in the medium, from sound effects operators to the stars of yesteryear. I had thoroughly enjoyed writing and researching it, and the book had sold quite well – but I regarded it as something of a prentice piece. Now I was working on another, this time about memories of Australian childhood. But fiction was what real writers wrote, I believed, and that meant a novel. Nothing much had changed from London, really – I still had ideas floating around in my head, though none of them had magically coalesced into an actual work. But that might happen soon, I thought, and I would be ready for it. Just as soon as I got rid of having to edit manuscripts for a living. At the same time I knew even then, I think, that the solitary life of the full-time writer was not for me: I found meeting people and working with them and with their words – which editing gave me – more satisfying than the kind of isolated intensity needed to write an actual novel.

I can see now that I was really not very different from all the other young Australian women who had been good at English at school, had gone to university, travelled a bit, collected a store of interesting anecdotes for the amusement of friends. True, I hadn't completed the other part of the usual story: I was in my late thirties without having married or had children. But as far as I was concerned that was fine, certainly not a cause for regret.

So here I was, a literary-minded and independent household of one. I had even developed a small reputation as the go-to person for an apt quotation or the title of a book. I liked lending my books to friends and talking about them; I usually remembered people's birthdays and enjoyed combing bookshops for books they might like – whether they were readers or not. So I lived in words, was surrounded by words; words were my business. My job was to manipulate them, sometimes, to put them in the best possible order so that the author's intention was clear. Clarity was the aim, and I liked to think that finding it was my skill, too. There were times, though, when this all felt rather secondhand. Sometimes, not often, I wondered whether I was like the woman in an early Margaret Drabble novel (*The Millstone*, I think) whose education had taught her to think mainly in quotations. When feeling melancholy, as I sometimes was, I wondered how much I really knew about the world.

It's very easy to get a name for independence of

mind when you don't really engage with the messiness of life. And this I think is exactly what I had done: I had shielded myself behind a wall of books and a regulated pattern of work, both immensely enjoyable, true, but removed from dispute and challenge except on a level I had chosen. I knew that there were potential dangers in living too much alone: the arthritis of habit or emotion could easily set in. However, I was never down for long. There was always a new manuscript that needed work, another idea about what I might write, and I was generally content with that.

One afternoon in February 1986 I was sorting through photographs for a book about horses when the phone rang. I clambered across piles of encyclopedias and notes and boxes of transparencies heaped on the floor and picked up, to find myself speaking to Margaret Gee, a small independent publisher I did not know and had never worked for. She explained that she needed an editor for a book of humorous bush stories she was publishing, and asked whether this was the sort of thing I liked working on.

My first impulse was to say no. Bush yarns, especially the broadly Australian, Bill Wannan stone-the-crows kind, I have always found pointless and tedious. I hadn't known that they were still being published. While I was forming a refusal in my mind, Margaret added, 'The book is called *The Killer Koala*, and the stories are written by Kenneth Cook ... have you heard of him?'

'Oh yes,' I said.

'Well, would you like to edit them? I don't think they need much work ...'

That's what they all say, I thought. But even so ...

'Sure,' I said.

Not long afterwards the phone rang again. On the other end were the rich modulated tones I recognised and remembered instantly. Kenneth Cook clearly had no recollection of our previous encounter, and his voice was on its best behaviour. 'Ms Kent,' he said, being very careful about the pronunciation of 'Ms', 'what I am about to say is very important to me. I am not used to being edited. My characters do not exclaim, they do not snort, wince in speech, respond, or chuckle or gibber. I don't want you to change "he said" or "she said" to any of these things. Is that clear?'

Oh, for ...

'Perfectly clear, thank you, Mr Cook,' I said, making no effort to keep the sarcasm out of my voice. 'And would you like me to put hyphens between the syllables of the long words, too?'

At the other end of the line there was a long – I hoped stunned – pause.

'I think we should have lunch,' he said.

I had assumed that we would meet in a pub bistro or a cheap and cheerful Asian restaurant somewhere in the inner city, so I was surprised when Ken suggested the Stationmaster's Cottage at St Leonards. It turned out to be a square sandstone house with frilly curtains and a cute little carriage lamp beside the front door, obviously dedicated to expense-account dining. It was utterly unlike my expectations of Kenneth Cook's taste. As I followed the black-clad maître d' past a set of colonial hunting prints on the wall, I wondered whether the man waiting for me at the table was a suit-wearing bizoid in disguise.

At first glance Ken Cook looked very much like the man I remembered. However, when I looked more closely the changes were obvious and a little disconcerting. He might have been insouciant about his head operation in print, but it had clearly taken its toll. His face was lined and thinner, his eyes deeply bagged, his curly hair now much greyer. He looked as if some air had leaked out of him. But his eyes were as green and penetrating as before, and the impudent twinkle I remembered from dinner at Clare's house was still there.

'Hello,' he said, as we shook hands. 'I think we've met before, haven't we. At Clare's?' So he did remember. 'I had a bit of a go at you, didn't I? Clearly that didn't work out.' No trace of embarrassment, I noticed; I was the one who felt a bit awkward. 'What are you drinking?'

On the snowy white tablecloth was a half-empty bottle of Riesling; he had apparently arrived some time before me, though I hadn't been late. Next to it was a stack of A4 paper held together by a rubber band. He tapped the pile carelessly. 'That's it,' he said. '*Killer Koala*. Stories.' He shrugged as if to say, *nothing much really*.

If working as an editor had taught me anything, it was that no writer on planet Earth truly believes that his or her work is *nothing much really*. 'I'll have a read and let you know,' I said.

'Yes, of course,' he said. 'You're the editor, you must do as you think fit.' He didn't sound convinced, so I asked him whether he had dealt directly with editors in the past. 'Only working for magazines, not for novels,' he said. 'I only agreed to have an editor for these stories because Margaret Gee told me I would probably need one. It's the way they do things now, apparently.' I spotted an attitude I had met before in older writers: *I have been writing for forty years, thanks very much, and I don't need somebody your age to tell me how to do it. I'll agree to an editor under sufferance, but leave my words alone.* I knew there was more than the simple resentment of allegedly know-it-all youth behind this, though that played a part. Incredible as it seemed to me and my contemporaries,

Ken's generation of Australian writers – Ruth Park, D'Arcy Niland, Elizabeth Harrower, Dal Stivens – had usually had their work presented to the reader almost exactly as it had been submitted to the publisher, with perhaps a bit of tweaking from a proofreader. I knew from experience that some authors declared they didn't mind their words being changed – as long as nothing was actually altered. I also knew that author–editor conflicts could blow up with the speed and intensity of a summer storm and take much longer to dissipate. I really hoped this wasn't going to happen here.

I asked Ken whether the *Killer Koala* stories had come from his own experience in the bush. 'Some of them,' he said. 'They're all based on fact, one way or another. I had fun writing them. There's forty years of experience behind them.' He was silent for a moment or two. Then he asked suddenly, 'Do you like this restaurant?'

'Yes, it's very nice,' I said politely.

He looked relieved. 'Good,' he said. 'It's not really my sort of place, but I'm glad you like it.' So he had chosen this place to please me, he had wanted to impress me? I had never met a man who would admit such a thing so frankly, and now I was wary that this might be intended as something more than a business lunch. When we ordered I found, as I suspected, that the dishes were quite expensive – by my standards anyway – and I decided that when the time came I would insist we split the bill.

I relaxed a bit over lunch, though slightly alarmed about the second bottle of wine that Ken insisted on ordering. It seemed he would rather drink and smoke than eat, for he constantly held a cigarette between thumb and middle finger and took quick, deep puffs before mashing it into the ashtray. It was my only clue that perhaps he was less assured than he looked. But I was hardly in a position to judge him for his love of nicotine – in those days I too was a smoker.

So we sat at our table and talked and smoked cigarettes and drank wine all afternoon. What did we talk about? When I look back I can see that of course we were testing each other. Ken spoke with feeling about the bush, especially the country in western New South Wales where he had shot wild pigs; he had also been tuna fishing in South Australia and mining for opals. He told me about these things matter-of-factly, not even attempting to project himself as a Hemingwayesque type. As he was wearing the same maroon jumper and grey trousers I had seen at Clare's, I couldn't imagine him drawing a bead on a charging feral pig or shooting kangaroos. Yet he clearly knew about these things; this was the man who had written *Wake in Fright* . . .

I found I had done more travelling than he, for he had been to London briefly, hardly anywhere in the rest of Europe, and only in the context of taking his wife and children on holiday years before, when the children were small. He apparently had no desire to travel for its own sake; he did not seek out museums or concert halls or famous bits of scenery anywhere in the world, it seemed. He listened politely while I spoke about my own travels and my time living in London, but his attitude was very clear: why bother to go anywhere else when there was so much that was unique and wonderful in Australia? He managed to get this across without a whiff of I'm-bloody-Australian-and-I'll-always-stand-up-for-bloody-Australia nationalism. This was an almost comic contrast to the weary hatred of the outback he had expressed in *Wake in Fright*. So what did he really think?

What also puzzled me was his attitude to the subject I had tacitly assumed was dearest to both our hearts: books and writing. I had assumed we would have an enjoyable and far-reaching discussion about Australian and other literature. Sure, I wasn't really expecting him to be up to speed with the feminist writers of the time – Anne Summers or Germaine Greer or Gloria Steinem – or the work of local feminist collective presses such as Sisters Publishing or Redress Press. After all, he was a bloke. But I had thought the work of Kate Grenville, Tim Winton, Robert Drewe, Murray Bail, Elizabeth Jolley, Helen Garner and/or

Frank Moorhouse would come up in conversation, and for him to have read their work and to have opinions about them. Apparently not.

One book he said he particularly liked was *God Knows* by Joseph Heller. I hadn't read it, and when he told me it was 'a sort of comic novel about King David' I didn't really feel keen about it, even though I had loved Heller's huge bestseller *Catch-22*. 'You really must read it,' he told me, and I said I would. Two of his favourite writers were Evelyn Waugh and, especially, Graham Greene. Yes, I agreed enthusiastically, *Scoop* was one of the great comic novels. I could even recite my favourite bit, Waugh's parody of the 'Nature Notes' so beloved of English newspaper columnists: 'Feather-footed through the plashy fen passes the questing vole.' He had forgotten that, and we laughed about it together. When he laughed his face creased into dozens of tiny lines and his contagious chuckle was deep and rumbling, with an almost choking quality. And speaking of quotations, he offered one of his favourites: 'Abroad is unutterably bloody and foreigners are fiends.'

'So you like Uncle Matthew?' I said, recognising Nancy Mitford's lunatic English lord from *The Pursuit of Love*. I got points for that, I could see. Then we got onto Kingsley Amis's *Lucky Jim* and agreed that it was one of the world's great comic novels. We both loved the Australian writer Lennie Lower ('I am perhaps a little under medium height, but then mere height is nothing. Notice the relative importance of Napoleon and the giraffe') and had both hugely enjoyed Max Gillies reading Lower's *Here's Luck* on ABC radio a couple of years before.

'Ah, the writing game,' he said, mashing yet another cigarette into the ashtray (which had been replaced by attentive waiters at least twice by now). 'The fun's gone out of it. There are other things to do, you know.'

'Like what?' I asked.

I believed that the business of true writers was solely to put words on paper. When I expressed a less idealistic version of this, his response was a slightly pitying look. 'You can't make a quid at it, not in this country,' he said. 'And you know, all writers ever think about is money.' He said this with airy self-confidence, with a challenging gleam in his eye that I later came to know as the invitation to an argument. I let it go, just asking – as no doubt he intended – what else he did besides write. And then, of all things, he started talking about insects.

They'd always fascinated him, he said – and so he started making short natural history films that he sold to the ABC, mainly for children. He was involved in a TV production company, Patrician Films, named after his wife Patricia, which went on to make kids' adventure stories, and he got his own children involved as extras. Making films did all right, he said – but he wanted to do more.

'So I set up an animal park,' he said. This was in the early 1970s, when Australia didn't have anything of the sort. Ken got some friends and financial backers together; they bought land near the Hawkesbury River out of Sydney and set up the Butterfly Farm. The centrepiece was a pavilion where people could see different species of butterfly, collected by enthusiasts in Queensland and northern New South Wales. There was a bull ants' nest behind glass and an insect museum, as well as the more obvious Australian animals, including wombats, echidnas and kangaroos. 'Some really strange characters turned up there,' he said. He tapped the manuscript on the table. 'I've written about a couple of them in here.'

I had never heard of the Butterfly Farm. Was Ken still involved in running it? I asked. 'No,' he said. 'It didn't do as well as we wanted. And then there were hundred-year floods on the Hawkesbury for two successive years.

'So we had to bail out. There was some messy winding up … the whole thing sent me broke,' he said.

'Oh. I'm sorry to hear that,' I said. He shrugged. 'The whole project was ahead of its time,' he said. 'Still, that's the way it goes. And it's only money.'

By now all the other diners had gone, shadows were

creeping across the lawn outside and the traffic on the Pacific Highway was reaching its peak-hour bellow. And all the time we were talking I was acutely conscious of his physicality, the way his mouth formed words, his voice, the quizzical arch of his eyebrows, the crooked middle finger of his right hand, his rumbling laughter. I wanted to stay in the Stationmaster's Cottage for a long time, I wanted him to tell more stories, I wanted to know more about him. The camaraderie between us made me think I had known him for years. A friendly bear. And of course I was well aware of the fizz of sexuality between us, a source of energy, not of tension.

As the waiters pointedly folded tablecloths and wiped down tables, we decided that we had better go. 'I'm paying my share,' I said, getting out my purse and making a quick calculation about the amount on my credit card. He looked at me blandly. 'But the bill's already settled,' he said.

I nearly said, *Well, my turn next time*, but just stopped myself. Was I assuming another lunch? I believed he had enjoyed the lunch as much as I had – and for similar reasons – but wary instinct told me not to push anything. So I simply said, 'Thank you.'

He offered me a lift home, which I accepted as I do not drive, and the idea of getting home after all that wine was a bit daunting. Though he had drunk more than I, he seemed completely unaffected – there were no booze buses in those days. I followed him to the car park and a battered red Honda Civic at least ten years old. Its registration sticker was attached to the window by a piece of duct tape, and the interior smelled fiercely of wet dog.

'Sorry about the smell,' said Ken as he clashed the gearstick and sent the car into reverse. 'It's George. My Alsatian. He often travels with me. Very useful to have a dog like him around when you go bush. Puts certain kinds of people off.'

We pulled up in front of Bellarion Court and he handed me the manuscript of *The Killer Koala*. I felt a little awkward as I thanked him for lunch once again, and arranged to call him after I had finished evaluating the stories. We shook hands for the second time that day, and he drove off, grinding the gears again.

I sat down to read *The Killer Koala* the following morning, still feeling the agreeable glow of our meeting. What would I say, I wondered, if these bush stories turned out to be flat and dull? Or if they were old-fashioned and laboured in a Dad-and-Dave bush-yarn style? I had responded to Ken's lightness of spirit and his sense of fun, but I knew there was no reason to suppose that humour in person works on the page.

I also knew that if I did not like *The Killer Koala* I would not be able to pretend I did. Ken, like any author, would spot lack of enthusiasm in a millisecond, no matter how I might try to disguise it. As I took the top page off the stack, I realised that I really wanted to like what he had written.

This is how the title story began:

> *I do not like koalas. They are nasty, cross, stupid creatures without a friendly bone in their bodies. Their social habits are appalling – the males are always beating their fellows up and stealing their females. They have disgusting defence mechanisms. Lice infest their fur. They snore. Their resemblance to cuddly toys is a base deceit. There is nothing to recommend them.*

This tone turned out to be fairly typical of the whole collection. Told in the first person like most bush yarns, the stories basically had one comic subject: the hapless, slightly effete city slicker faced with the bloody-mindedness of Australia's native fauna that, to a kangaroo and an echidna, is determined to do him in.

As Ken had told me during lunch, the Butterfly Farm featured in a couple of the stories. I particularly liked Vic the Snake Man, surname unknown, who ran a show featuring snakes and other venomous creatures, which he handled with supreme nonchalance. He was hugely popular, wrote Ken, largely because all the kids who came to watch the show were waiting for him to be bitten and die. But his great boast was that no snake would ever hurt him because he understood them so well. Then one day a tiger snake reared up and struck Vic on the hand three times. The audience gasped, thrilled, but Vic only swore and sucked his hand. He called a young boy out of the audience to get him a pint of milk, drank that straight down and went on with the show. About an hour after he finished he collapsed – keeled over stiff as a board, Ken wrote – and was rushed to hospital. He was unable to speak or move for a long time, though he did recover. However, he had nothing more to do with snakes after that.

The *Killer Koala* stories were light-hearted and fun, and they read effortlessly. However, I knew enough about writing to be aware that they showed considerable craft. It wasn't just that the jokes were good. Being funny in print involves rhythm and timing, skills that take years to learn. I found myself wondering whether Ken read his words aloud to himself, as I knew some writers did. And I could have laid bets that he had written for radio at some point, like most writers of his vintage: the cadences and the pace were very suited to spoken word.

And this was the work of the man who had written

the grimly nihilistic *Wake in Fright*? But after a little thought I could see how the two books were connected. Both featured a naïve city-based man confronting life in the bush and coming out badly – though in the stories the agents of destruction were the animals of the Australian bush rather than the people. There was no similarity in tone, to put it mildly, but it wasn't too much of a stretch to see that the *Killer Koala* stories were the funny flip side of *Wake in Fright*.

The manuscript had been impeccably typed, and there wasn't much editorial work for me to do – just minor fixing of punctuation. The whole editorial process took less than two days. When I had finished I called Ken and asked him to come to my place so we could go through the manuscript together. Normally I would have handed the edited manuscript to an author without further comment, and probably via the publisher, but I told myself that if Ken had had little experience of editing and editors, direct contact would probably be a good idea. Of course I knew that this was an excellent way of making sure I saw him again.

And so one morning not long afterwards we sat side by side at my small kitchen table, the manuscript between us. Ken's physicality seemed more insistent than at the restaurant: his presence made my apartment seem smaller than ever. I began to go through the manuscript page by page, but before very long his shoulders began to sag. He started to slouch in his seat and stare into space like a bored schoolboy.

'I hate rereading my stuff,' he said. 'Let's not spend any more time on this. I can see what you've done, I trust you. Can't we leave it at that?' Sure, I said. He looked satisfied, and asked me what I was doing for the rest of the day. As I had planned to spend the next couple of hours going through the stories, I was at a loose end – nothing much, I told him. 'Excellent,' he said. 'Then let's go for a walk.' He suggested we go to Forty Baskets Beach on the edge of Manly, but on the way he had to stop home to collect George the dog, who hadn't had a walk that day.

Half an hour later Ken's Honda Civic was buzzing down Military Road and over the Spit Bridge like an eager red wasp. As he drove, his right elbow sticking out of the driver's window in defiance of the rules of the road, he explained that he lived in the same house as his four adult children, one of whom was married with a small daughter. When he and Patricia split up they had sold the family home and Patricia moved into a unit, where she now lived. Ken had seen an old and shabby two-storeyed house in James Street, Manly, not too far from Patricia. He bought it for a good price and had it made into four apartments, each on a separate title, one for each of his children. Three of them – Megan, Kerry and Paul – now lived there, he explained, and he was in the fourth, which technically belonged to Anthony, who preferred to live elsewhere. 'It was one of my best deals,' he said.

This living arrangement was a kind of family closeness beyond anything I had ever seen or known about. I guessed that Ken's children must be in their twenties, working, and mostly single. What were they doing, still living with their father? In my world, you left the parental home as soon as you could afford to be independent. As we drove past neat brick houses and gardens full of oleanders and banksias, I wondered what it was that tied Ken and his children so closely together.

THE WRITING LIFE

We stopped outside a brick building in a quiet street. I followed Ken past the sugar gum in the front garden and round the back, where we climbed up a wooden staircase to a landing on the first floor with two facing doors. Ken unlocked the door on the right and we stepped into what was obviously a living room. There was hardly any furniture in it: two wooden chairs, a small and delicate table that looked antique and that I guessed he had taken from the family home. Close to the window was, of all things, a table-tennis table with the net up. There was seagrass matting on the floor, the reason why the whole room smelled powerfully like chicken feed.

To the right was a small kitchen. The stove looked suspiciously clean, as if nobody did any actual cooking on it. Open shelves above the sink held a collection of glasses, some apparently salvaged from pubs, and a slotted plastic tray with an assortment of cutlery. There was also a tiny fridge that I suspected held beer rather than fresh green vegetables.

Living area and kitchen both looked hastily put together, as if the owner had dumped what was needed for the time being and was just camping there on his way to somewhere more interesting. This certainly chimed with the restlessness I had noticed in Ken that night at Clare's. What struck me too was that there were no pens, stacks of paper, notebooks or typewriter: nothing suggested that this was the room of a writer. True, against one wall was a wooden bookcase crammed with books, but they seemed to be paperback popular novels. I picked out *Lucky Jim*, a couple of Graham Greenes and several books by Winston Graham, an author I didn't know. I guessed these were the books Ken liked having with him on his travels. But I saw few staples of a writer's library: dictionaries, thesauruses, reference books about birds or animals or Australian history. He had a small dog-eared copy of the *Macquarie Dictionary* and a paperback *Oxford*, but that was all. So where was he working on the couple of projects he had mentioned at Clare's? Was he doing any literary work at all?

On one shelf was a chunk of rock about five centimetres square. 'Here,' said Ken, and he picked it up and handed it to me. 'Take a look at this.' I took it and turned it over, and the rock flashed green and blue. I held in my hand the opal bones of the continent of Australia, formed millions of years ago beneath the sea. 'It's from White Cliffs, not far from Wilcannia,' he said.

Ken explained that this particular piece of opal was a 'good' one. Sometimes, he said, when you turn opal stone to the light you can see a golden streak running through it about as wide as a hair. 'That's called a ginger whisker,' he said. 'If you try and cut any opal stone that has this flaw, it will shatter.' Something about the serious way he said this made me think it was more than just an interesting piece of geological information. And indeed he explained that the town in his novel *The Man Underground*, featuring various dodgy characters who mined for opal, was named – with the whoosh of a metaphor coming in to land – Ginger Whisker.

'My works,' said Ken, waving a nonchalant hand at the bookcase. I took another look and saw now that the top shelf held seven or eight paperback novels with his name on the spine; others were by Alan Hale and John Duffy, authors unknown to me. Ken explained that these were pseudonyms of his. *The Take* by John Duffy, which was fairly typical of these novels, had on the cover a glamorous brunette holding a champagne glass and naked to the waist except for coyly breast-covering elbow-length red gloves. 'The outrageously wicked story of a passionate dusky damsel who wants to be naughty and very often succeeds,' was the cover line. I recognised the publisher: Horwitz, an Australian publisher well known for cheap paperbacks of violent melodrama and knock-offs of Raymond Chandler detective stories. *The Take* had been published in 1963, only two years after *Wake in Fright*. Had it really been necessary for him to write this stuff after such a successful book? When I asked Ken this – a little more diplomatically – he gave me a rueful smile. '*Wake in Fright* didn't do all that well at first,' he said. 'I don't love these books, but you do what you must to earn a quid.' So, I thought, this was life for a successful Australian writer in the 1960s.

There were translations too: editions of *Wake in Fright* in Japanese, Chinese, Russian and German, all with dull buff or grey covers, like old textbooks. I wondered what their readers made of John Grant's beer-sodden humiliation in outback Australia. 'I've never made anything much from translations,' said Ken, echoing a complaint I had heard from other writers. 'All the fame and no bloody money, as they used to say.'

I checked over the other shelves, finding several of Ken's novels I had never heard of. One was *Eliza Fraser*, clearly produced to capitalise on a mid-1970s movie of the same name, since it showed the pretty blonde English film star Susannah York on the cover. I vaguely remembered that the story was about a young woman shipwrecked off the Queensland coast in the 1830s, who lived for a while with the Indigenous people. *A Fringe of Leaves* by Patrick White, with the same subject, had been published at about the same time, I realised. When I mentioned this, Ken snorted. Obviously he was not a White fan. He told me his book had been modelled on the Flashman series by George MacDonald Fraser, another novelist he admired. 'Sold really well, my book did,' said Ken with relish. 'Right up until the movie was released. Then it sank like a stone.' Another standout on the shelf was a thick paperback with the odd title of *The Wine of God's Anger* and a cover depicting a grim-faced soldier wearing a Vietnam-era helmet. A young conscript's awful experiences in battle, according to the blurb. It wasn't difficult to see another echo of *Wake in Fright*, another story of a young man's nightmare in an alien world. 'Wrote that at the end of the sixties,' said Ken. 'It's still the only Australian novel about the Vietnam War.'

The covers of some of the other books on the shelf were spectacular, and not in a good way. *Bloodhouse* had a photograph of a sledgehammer covered in thick red goo and oozing over a green background, *Tuna* featured a large silver fish impaled on a gaff, *Stormalong* a swirling and dangerous-looking whirlpool. I was surprised to see that the publisher for all of these was Michael Joseph, a UK imprint I had always associated with good-quality popular fiction; these trashy covers made Ken's books look like rubbish. Worst of the lot was their UK hardback edition of *Wake in Fright*, its title in straggly blood-red letters above a skinny stick figure, also in red, against a viciously mustard-yellow background. It was one of the ugliest book jackets I had ever seen, and I wondered whether the designer had even bothered to read the book. Were these so badly presented, I wondered, because they were the work of an Australian writer – books a British publisher didn't need to bother with because they probably wouldn't have sold well in the UK market? It certainly seemed so.

I picked up this edition of *Wake in Fright* and searched for the scene I most vividly remembered: the long description of the kangaroo shoot that propels John Grant into his worst excesses.

> *As Grant's eager finger worked to reload he could hear the tearing thump the bullets made as they hit flesh. And presently the kangaroos began to fall down, even in the act of dying keeping their heads turned to the great mass of light that had burst from the bush to become the last thing they would see …*

The passage was as powerful and sickening as it had been the first time I read it. How had readers and reviewers reacted in England, where the love of animals was legendary? Much later, when I came to look up English reviews, I discovered to my surprise that the brutal scene barely rated a mention by the London critics. *Wake in Fright*'s reviews described it as a rite-of-passage story. Maybe reviewers had assumed that all Australians treated their native fauna in this horrible way.

As I stood by the bookcase, leafing through *Wake in Fright* in that ramshackle Manly flat, I recognised a quality in Ken I had glimpsed all those months ago at Clare's party. The writing was clear, flowing and apparently effortless, but behind it was something much harder, something implacable. And that day, when Ken explained how he came to write *Wake in Fright,* I understood why.

He told me that he had left school in Sydney just before the end of the war, a robust fifteen-year-old Irishman ready to take on the world. His weapons were unbounded confidence, good looks (he was tall with green eyes and black hair), charm, a bright quick mind and a way with words. He talked his way into a cadetship on the *Richmond River Express*, based in Casino in northern New South Wales, and for the next few years he moved around the state on country papers, covering cattle and sheep sales, CWA meetings, weather reports, farming equipment. But he longed to get back to the city.

Finally he landed a job with the ABC as a radio journalist, married Patricia Hickie, a librarian, when he was not quite twenty-two and she was twenty, and they started a family. The young Cooks moved around various country towns and before long Ken was chafing under the restrictions of journalism. But he could not afford to leave a steady job – Patricia had given up work when she married and they had two small daughters – and so he freelanced at night and on weekends, mostly writing radio scripts and moonlighting for rural newspapers as a journalist and occasional short-story writer – all under a variety of pseudonyms, since he was supposed to work only for the ABC.

To make a living as a freelance writer, speed and flexibility were essential. Ken's experience as a journalist, as well as his temperament, had taught him about both and he was always quick to learn more. But he wanted to write novels, which took up more time than the other work he was doing – and he was lucky enough to have the kind of steady job that would help to pay for his time. He was drawn to realistic stories set in country Australia, perhaps involving shady characters, and when he was sent to Rockhampton for the ABC he found a subject ready to hand.

'This wasn't what became *Wake in Fright*,' he said. 'I had to cover a trial involving a well-known local bloke. This character was up to his eyeballs in anything that was going: brothels, organised crime, fixing horse races, you name it. Wonderful stuff. I was taking all this down in shorthand in the court and thinking what a terrific novel this would make.' He wrote up the story of the court case, with its principals heavily disguised, and called his novel *Vantage to the Gale*.

Ken knew that to make his mark he had to be published by a UK-based publishing house. He sent his manuscript to Hodder and Stoughton, whose popular fiction list had an established presence in Australia. A couple of months later he was notified by post that Hodder had accepted *Vantage to the Gale*. Ken told me that opening and reading that letter marked the happiest day of his life. He knew he wouldn't get rich – the print run, which would be sold back to Australia, was small and he would receive a 'colonial' royalty (that is, one not based on the book's selling price but on a proportion of the publisher's receipts, which was a much lesser amount). But this did not worry him. He was on his way, and full of confidence that the money would roll in later.

But the Rockhampton court case was still dragging on, with little sign of finishing before publication. The Australian distributors grew alarmed and Hodder had the manuscript checked for libel. Lawyers decided that the plot was too close to the bone. But even worse than that: Ken, drawing on his memory, had unwittingly included material that closely echoed the court transcripts. Crossly, Hodder and Stoughton decided to abandon publication. And so, overnight, Kenneth Cook became a promising young novelist without a book to his name. The blow was devastating.

Ken was thirty: he had made a pact with himself to give up journalism when he reached that age and to write novels full-time. That dream – hardly a realistic one – had now evaporated. Back in Sydney for the ABC, with Patricia and now three young children, shortly to be four, Ken and the family were living in a cheap flat in Narrabeen on the northern beaches about twenty kilometres from the city. Ken travelled to work at the ABC news office in Kings Cross by motorbike, putting sheets of newspaper inside his jumper to keep out the wind as he barrelled along Pittwater Road. For extra money he and a mate ran a boat business in Elizabeth Bay on weekends.

But Ken had another idea for a novel that was aching to be written. 'You don't *decide* on a novel. It just happens to you, it grabs you by the balls and you have to get it down,' he told me. This one was about a young, naïve teacher and his five-day nightmare in and around an outback town called Bundanyabba, an amalgam of several towns in Queensland and New South Wales Ken had known as a rural journalist. Writing on the kitchen table in an exercise book after the rest of the family was in bed, with cigarettes and whisky his only companions, he finished *Wake in Fright*, he told me, in less than two months. In so doing, Ken established a pattern of work he followed for the rest of his writing life: once he had an idea and had worked out a plot – however long all that took – he sat down and wrote the story straight away. He had the manuscript typed by a family friend and sent it off to Michael Joseph. They accepted it, did almost no editing to the text and published it for the UK and Australian markets in 1961. Ken was thirty-two.

Wake in Fright was his essential stroke of luck, the calling card that every young writer needs, and Ken took full advantage of it. Always and forever scornful of the safe option, convinced with William Blake that *the tigers of wrath are wiser than the horses of instruction*, he left the ABC and began to write full-time, calculating that he could use income from his further novels as collateral (which explained the quickie pulp thrillers I had seen). This, he thought, was the path to success, and for a lot of the time it was. When several film producers wanted to make a film of *Wake in Fright*, he was delighted to accept the option money, even though most of these deals fizzled out. And then in 1968 he was approached for the film rights by none other than his fellow Australian novelist Morris West.

I knew West as the exceedingly successful author

of several novels, including *The Devil's Advocate* and *The Shoes of the Fisherman*, both made into movies. 'He was very conscious of his success, was Morris,' Ken told me. 'He liked to be considered a great writer, which I thought was a bit much. He would ask you over, and you'd go into the living room and shuffle across a mile of carpet that came up to your knees. He'd be standing next to a marble plinth with a light perpetual shining upon a copy of *The Devil's Advocate*, and you were supposed to bend the knee in homage to it while Morris smiled on you.'

When *Wake in Fright* was about to be published in the USA, Ken asked West to write a cover line endorsing it. West refused. He hated the ending, he said. Grant should not have been allowed to resume his former life, he should have accepted the depths of degradation to which he had descended. According to Ken, West agreed to write the cover line only if Grant did not survive at the end of the novel.

Ken refused, of course, but West was still flatteringly interested in optioning *Wake in Fright* for a movie. Ken said he was paid $6000 for the rights – a reasonable figure in the late 1960s – and the option was renewed a couple of times. Then a few years later he discovered that West had onsold the rights to Westinghouse Broadcasting, in partnership with the Australian company NLT, for a lot of money, and the movie duly went ahead. Ken told me West made about $50,000 out of the deal. 'All I ever made from the movie of *Wake in Fright* was the option money.'

Whatever the ethics of what West had done, he had acted within the law: the original option contract had been sloppily worded. Ken, inexperienced and never known as a stickler for this kind of detail, had signed cheerfully because, he said, he assumed that this option would be like all the others and the movie would never be made.

This was a story that Ken often told, I discovered, and he cheerfully blackened West's reputation whenever he could. He usually finished by saying something like, 'I learned something about the film industry after that ... and I learned even more about Morris bloody West.' Hard lessons.

Behind me, in the flat, I heard a bark that was almost a squeal. From what I assumed was the bedroom an enormous Alsatian was padding towards me, all grey and black fur, shrewd yellow eyes and glistening teeth. I glanced nervously towards the door.

'This is George,' said Ken. He bestowed a pat on the dog's massive flank. 'Say hello to Jacqueline, George.' The beast growled softly and gave me a level amber stare. Then, to my surprise, he plonked himself heavily on Ken's feet and presented his ears to be scratched. After Ken had obliged, George proceeded to lick his master's hand with such adoration – *thank you thank you kind master you are wonderful I love you* – that I started to feel slightly ill. No way was this creature the Hound of the Baskervilles. George was nothing but a canine Uriah Heep.

'Nobody's scared of George,' said Ken. 'Well, Sophie my granddaughter is, she's three. Everybody else loves him.' I wondered whether everybody else included Sophie's mother. George looked expectantly at Ken: *Walk? Yes?* But the sunlight had disappeared, the light through the window was greyish and a moment later there was a scatter-shot of rain on the window.

'Blast,' said Ken. 'Well, that takes care of our walk. Sorry, George.' He turned to me. 'Fancy a game of table tennis? Do you play?'

'A bit,' I said cautiously. 'Haven't for ages.' In fact my father had taught me the game when I was a child and I had played in teams at university, but not since then. Ken fished a couple of bats and a pingpong ball from behind the bookcase. 'I play a lot with my sons,' he told me, adding complacently, 'You'll find I'm pretty good.'

We faced each other at opposite ends of the table. Ken threw me the ball and I served, and we batted it back and forth. I was pleased to discover that even after almost twenty years I still knew how to flick the ball and how to judge the length of a shot. Ken went easy on me at first, as I had thought he might. But when he saw that I was winning, and fairly quickly at that, he started to play hard, going for reckless would-be killer shots that smashed the ball into the net or made it fly right off the table. Once the ball hit George, who whined in protest. I won the first game easily.

'Another one,' said Ken.

'Sure.' All through my teenage years my mother had told me that a smart woman always allowed a man to win any competition, even if she was better than he was – if she didn't, he wouldn't want to know her (and then where would she be?). It was advice I had ignored then, and I ignored it now.

'Twenty-one, seven,' I said, trying not to sound too smug.

'All right,' snapped Ken. 'Best of five.' It was his turn to serve. The ball hit the top of the net and dribbled back onto his side of the table. 'Blast!'

I won that game too. Not to put too fine a point upon it, I thrashed him.

'Best of seven.' He scowled at me.

I beamed upon him. 'Who are you, the Black Knight?'

He got the Monty Python reference, as I had hoped. 'All right,' he said, putting the bat down. 'You win.'

'There, there.' In Churchill's words, I was in defeat magnanimous, in victory insufferable. And because I was feeling cheerful and was pleased that I had made him behave like a sulky teenager, and I liked him very much and it felt right, I walked up to his end of the table and gave him a hug and a peck on the cheek. His beard was soft and he smelled of smoke and Palmolive soap.

'Oh dear,' he said softly.

At first I thought he was telling me that I shouldn't have done that. But I didn't feel in the least apologetic – it had been a spontaneously affectionate gesture, nothing more. But I looked at him and could see, no, that wasn't what he had meant – and now I admitted to myself that it hadn't quite been what I meant either. With that single careless, impulsive act I had opened a door to something more than a cheerful friendship. For me, the air was charged with possibility, and I could see that he thought so too.

I needed to get home, perhaps to think over what had just happened between us. The rain stopped a few minutes later, and I think we were both relieved. He drove me back to Bellarion Court and we hardly exchanged a word. There isn't really a lot you can say when you're at the beginning of a story and you aren't quite sure what will happen next.

CONVERSATIONS

My job as editor of Ken's short stories had come to an end. I had corrected the page proofs and sent them back to Margaret Gee. I was glad that stage had passed without animosity on Ken's part – when a book is typeset and looks more or less as it will in print, it's not uncommon for an author to lash out with a panic-stricken biro and change large swathes of the text. But Ken displayed very little interest in what his words would look like on the printed page, and he certainly showed no signs of wanting to read his work again. I could see that he didn't really care about the various stages of getting his book between covers; as long as it turned up with his name on it in a bookshop and people bought it, he was happy.

So now there was nothing left for me to do. I have often found this author–editor separation to be something of an anticlimax, even rather dismal. Here you are, intensely involved with each other for a few weeks, or months – with constant phone calls, messages, arguments about details of language and whether a passage needs to be extended or cut. Whether you end up friends or foes, there is always a certain kind of intimacy: you learn a lot about each other very quickly. Then, suddenly, the relationship is broken. When the finished book appears you might get a gracious mention as editor somewhere in the acknowledgements if the author feels kindly towards your collaboration. (This can be a double-edged sword: one editor I know was thanked by an author for 'treating this book as if it were her own'.) Ken and I had not had this kind of intense collaboration over his words, but for other reasons I knew I didn't want to lose him.

Evidently he felt as I did, because he suggested that we go for a walk on the next fine day. And so began our Manly bushwalks, once or twice a week. Whenever I think of this time, I see Ken slouching rapidly along a track in baggy jeans and joggers and a green short-sleeved shirt with the handy pocket for cigarette butts, and George trotting ahead. Our usual route took us through clumps of angophoras, their branches twisted like trees in paintings by Sydney Long, and past an almost deserted beach. We would walk until the scrub enclosed us, our only witnesses the small birds fluttering in the casuarinas. For a little while it was possible to believe – if we ignored the roof lines and the occasional overhead wire – that we were a long way from the city. Ken knew much more about the flora of the area than I did – most of my knowledge had been gleaned from editing books on botany, and I hadn't retained much – and he obviously knew and loved this part of the world, and was at peace within it. We never said much to each other on those walks, we were just together, in easy unity. I loved those times in the bush.

However, I was less keen on Ken's other preferred recreation: going to restaurants for dinner. He always chose gastronomic clones of the Stationmaster's Cottage, even though he had told me during that first lunch that he wasn't keen on that kind of upmarket restaurant. More than once, as I gloomily made my way through chicken smothered in thick light-reflecting sauce, enduring Barry Manilow in the background, I wished I had told him that this wasn't really the sort of place I liked either; he apparently still thought it was. I had another grievance, as every time we went out to dinner Ken adroitly sorted out the matter of the bill when I wasn't looking. My objections were always met with a look of bland innocence, an expression I came to know very well. Not only was this irritating in terms of an equality I felt I was being denied, but – as much to the point – I never got to choose where we ate.

In other ways, though, being with him was just so easy. Occasionally I reminded myself what gaps there were between us, in terms of life and literary experience. I had been born during Australia's prosperous years after World War II; I had moved smoothly through school and university, got a degree, travelled overseas on a shoestring, found interesting jobs without much trouble. He had known hard times, grown up during a depression and a war, knew the country where I had always worked in the city, was a seasoned writer of novels whereas I had published just one book. We knew some of the same people – the literary community was a very small world – but my generation of writers were literally closed books to him. As time passed, however, so did my initial feeling that we were from different generations. We just liked each other's company.

I think this was because Ken, as well as being fun to be with, was an intensely curious person, always asking questions – what was my political affiliation, did I have a religious sense, what was it like being the eldest of three girls? He took in whatever I said, and remembered it. This was a new experience for me: most men I had known would far rather have talked than listened. But at Clare's that night Ken had also been amused by my joke at his expense. He hadn't given me the impression that women were not supposed to make jokes, as the others had done. (Even the pleasant man who had been my companion that evening didn't always approve of this aspect of my character.) So that was encouraging. So was the fact that in none of our conversations, then and later, did Ken ever utter the fatal words, 'What do you mean?'

Even so, we didn't have quite the same sense of humour, though we were learning how to make each other laugh. I liked epigrammatic wit; his stock in trade was telling stories. They were always good, too, and often self-deprecating. After one dinner during his engagement to Clare, he said, she had produced a pretty blue and white china bowl filled with bunches of green grapes in iced water, and had placed a pair of small silver scissors beside it. The guests obediently snipped a few grapes off the bunch and put them on their side plates. Ken thought grape scissors, which he had never seen before, were effete and ridiculous. When it came to his turn, he hauled the dripping fruit out of the bowl and made to wrench off a bunch with his fingers. 'This took a bit of work,' he said. 'I had to pull hard. The bunch just exploded. There were grapes whining past people's heads like bullets. They were ducking all over the place.'

My favourite, however, was the story about the kangaroo named Les who found his way to the local brewery and plunged his snout into a pool of hops mash. 'A case of instant alcohol addiction,' said Ken.

The kangaroo's owner, an old man named Benny, burst into tears and pleaded with Les to pull himself together and give up the drink. Nothing doing: the kangaroo, drunk and spoiling for a fight, caused mayhem all over town.

Were these stories true? Who cared? I was quite happy to listen and to laugh. And occasionally I got my own back. Once I suggested, straight-faced, that he should make a lot of money by writing about feminism using Australian animals as characters. 'You could set it in a colony of brolgas,' I suggested. 'Or wallabies. And then one day, they meet this horse – or some other introduced species, male of course, large and feral and nasty ... sort of *Animal Farm*, only with Australian animals.'

He digested this in silence, and I could see him thinking, *Well, if this kind of thing is important to her I suppose I'd better go along with it*. 'Don't you think that'd work?' I said, helpfully.

'I don't think it's me,' he said.

He never guessed that I was winding him up, and I never told him.

We didn't always tell jokes or stories. I was pleased to discover during these conversations that he had fought against Australia's involvement in the war in Vietnam in the early 1970s, largely because Paul and Anthony were teenagers with an excellent chance of being conscripted if the war went on for a few more years. By this time he was a well-known writer, and he wanted to do more than write angry letters to *The Catholic Weekly* or *The Sydney Morning Herald*. As well as writing his anti-Vietnam novel *The Wine of God's Anger*, he went into politics as a member of Gordon Barton's Liberal Reform Group. I was surprised he hadn't joined the ALP, but at the time the Labor Party was strongly working-class and almost entirely union-dominated – not the largely middle-class party it became under Whitlam a few years later. In the 1960s the ALP wasn't the party that upwardly mobile people felt represented them – and as I was soon to discover, Ken had devoted considerable energy to escaping from his working-class background in pursuit of a comfortable middle-class life. But unlike many of his friends he could never bring himself to vote Liberal because of the Vietnam issue, and he agreed with the LRG desire to split the Liberal Party vote by concentrating on opposition to Vietnam. He and Gordon Barton liked each other: they were both chancers, men of considerable energy and intelligence who were keen to have a go at rattling the cage when it suited.

Ken stood for Parliament in two successive federal elections (1966 and 1969), each time in a conservative seat, first for the LRG and later for Gordon Barton's Australia Party, and was crestfallen when his share of the vote only just topped six per cent both times. I wasn't surprised that he didn't do well, as I couldn't see him uttering platitudes in a town hall or handing out how-to-vote cards outside railway stations. I guessed that he wasn't the kind of person who enjoyed having to be nice to people he didn't know just so they would vote for him. I could tell, too, that he wasn't sold on a political career, and the slow and patient building of support wasn't something he enjoyed. Under his confidence, I was learning, lurked a streak of diffidence, and he wasn't the most patient person in the world either. After his failure to be elected he decided politics was a waste of time, and that the Australia Party didn't have enough fire in its belly. His disillusionment even extended to vegetables: he hated zucchini, which, he said, was such a bland, boring marrow that it could have been invented by the Australia Party.

Every time we parted Ken gave me a hug and a chaste goodnight kiss on the cheek. We had been seeing each other for several weeks now. I knew I hadn't been mistaken about the fizz of sexuality between us – I found him attractive, presumably he felt the same way about me and this had been true from our first lunch together – so why, I asked myself, was he not making any moves on me? I told myself that it was refreshing not to have to deal with that, but I was puzzled nevertheless. Still, if undemanding friendship and companionship were all he wanted from me, that was fine too. Sort of.

Easter was approaching, and I had made no plans. I assumed that we would probably go for a walk if the weather was fine, and maybe have lunch or dinner somewhere. So when he called me before the holiday weekend I was cheerfully casual. It was only when he said he wanted to talk to me about something that I realised his voice had become uncharacteristically serious.

He said, 'I don't quite know how to say this, but I'll say it anyway. I don't want us to go on as we are.'

This was the last thing I had expected, and I was surprised to realise what a blow it was.

'Are you saying you don't want us to see each other any more?' I asked.

'That's entirely up to you,' he said. 'Look, I enjoy your company …'

'And I enjoy yours too,' I told him.

'But I think we should call it quits, unless …'

'Unless what?'

'Well, this isn't really going anywhere,' he said.

'I see. Since when has our association been a train or a bus?'

'Very witty, Jacqueline. Tell you what. Today's Thursday. I won't see you over the Easter weekend. If you want to go on with this, take it to the next stage, call me on Monday. Is that OK?'

So from then on, whatever happened – or did not – was my decision. Looking back now, I can see how smart he was.

'All right,' I said. And I said goodbye, feeling blank.

On that Easter weekend my eighty-nine-year-old grandmother died, after battling emphysema for years. I spent a lot of time on the phone to my sister, aunt and cousins as we remembered who she was and what she had meant to us all. There was so much: the phone calls that always started with 'Hello, darling, it's only Nan', the Five Flavors Life Savers she always gave us as kids, her lemon sponge cakes, the liver and bacon that nobody else made so well, her pride in having hair that remained brown to the end of her life. How she had come into her own after our grandfather died; her visit to London while I was living there, the only overseas trip she ever made, and her reverent silence in front of the waxwork of Agatha Christie at Madame Tussauds: 'What wonderful thoughts!' she said. Her hugs; her deep, chesty chuckle. And one memory in particular that always made me smile, the day I told her about my first book, the oral history of Australian radio. 'You've written a book?' she said. 'How much did you have to pay to get it published?' I explained how standard book publishing worked, with contracts and advances, and she said, 'They're paying you? To write a book?' her voice brimming with incredulity.

When I remembered that last thing I knew exactly who would enjoy that story, and I very nearly called to tell him. But I still hadn't decided what to do, so I didn't. And then came the evening of Easter Sunday. It was a cold night and I was at home alone, feeling raw about Nan, about a whole section of my childhood gone forever. Those memories brought forth other older and deeper griefs and I thought, *Bugger it. Life is short.* And I picked up the phone and dialled Ken's number before I could change my mind.

He answered on the first ring. 'Hello?'

'Um, it's me,' I said, and I told him about Nan. He was concerned and sympathetic, as I knew he would be, and he chuckled over the story of the book, as I had hoped.

I took a deep breath. 'Look, I'm calling because … I know I said I'd call you on Monday, but I think it's probably Monday somewhere in the world, maybe Tierra del Fuego … so … anyway.'

'Ah,' he said. 'Excellent.' He sounded happy.

We didn't talk for long, and arranged to meet again soon. After I put the phone down I waited to feel pleased. But even though I knew I had been right, and that going on with this was what I wanted, I didn't feel as elated as I thought I should. And then I thought of something that had happened years before, when I was touring the Lake District. I went climbing up one of the fells by myself, feeling on top of the world. And then my feet had slipped on the scree and I skidded several metres down a slope. I had remained upright, my heart beating wildly, but that plunge downwards, though it had lasted only a few seconds, felt as if it would go on forever. I had had no idea how long the slide would last, or where or how it would end. What I felt now was that elation, and that fear.

OUT OF THE DARK

We lay in my bed together, with Ken's arm around my shoulders. I gazed at the play of watery light on the ceiling and listened to the fruit bats chittering to each other in the huge Moreton Bay fig outside the window. This was the time when I wanted us to talk to each other directly, intimately, perhaps telling secrets, recalling and sometimes laughing about things that had happened when we were kids, or perhaps at other times.

'When I was growing up, Mr Reed next door had a rooster that he called Leicester Square,' I said.

'Hmmm?'

'To remind him of Home.'

Ken chuckled about Mr Reed, but I soon realised that he was not going to tell any stories of his own. I tried to encourage him to talk about his early life by telling other anecdotes about the *sturm und drang* of my childhood in suburban Sydney – the time I ran away from home aged five and was rescued by a policeman and how furious I was; writing my first novel at the age of eleven on the letterhead of the EasiRain Automatic Sprinkler Co, a legacy of one of Dad's unsuccessful business ventures; the tale of our beloved miniature fox terrier named Menzies. I was surprised and perhaps crestfallen that Ken never joined in with stories about his own early life. Most men I knew were happy to talk about themselves as children, to look back on the boys they had been, often with affection.

One Saturday afternoon he came over and discovered me rereading George Johnston's *My Brother Jack*, a novel I had always liked. 'You enjoy that book, do you?' he asked. I told him I really admired Johnston's detailed evocation of Melbourne poverty during the Depression, I liked and understood the characters, and so on. He just grunted. 'It's not a bloody novel,' he said. 'I don't know why anybody ever thought it was. Johnston didn't do anything with his material. He just wrote down what happened. There's no invention, there's no attempt to make a story out of it. It's reportage, not fiction, nothing but journalism.'

'Why shouldn't George Johnston write about all that?' I asked. 'It was his life, it's stuff he knew. Are you saying that people shouldn't write novels about their own lives? That's ridiculous.'

‘Of course not,’ he said. ‘But why would I want to read all that stuff about family fights and brutality and dirt and poverty? It’s bloody boring. Nobody needs to write about those things.’

At first I put Ken’s irritation down to writerly competitiveness. *My Brother Jack* had been published three years after *Wake in Fright*, had won prizes and was widely praised: it had even been hailed as the Great Australian Novel. There might have been an element of that, of course, but I soon learned that Ken’s reaction was more personal than his scorn for Johnston as a storyteller.

A couple of weeks later he gave me a copy of a book he insisted I should read – *The Walking Stick* by Winston Graham. When I opened it a photograph fell out. It had clearly been taken by a street photographer and the clothes told me that it dated from the 1940s. Beaming out of the picture was a stocky woman in a long dark coat, sensible squat-heeled shoes and socks and no hat, carrying a huge handbag. She was not pretty, with a snub nose and wild, dark curly hair that looked as if she had slicked it into submission. But she had something more interesting than good looks – a force of personality that leapt out of the picture. And with her thick dark eyebrows and a mischievous smile that creased her face into a mass of tiny wrinkles, she looked startlingly familiar.

'Let me guess who this is,' I said.

Ken glanced at the photograph. 'That's Lily,' he said. 'My mother.'

'What was she like?'

He looked surprised that I should ask. 'She had a

bloody hard life for a long time, keeping the family together,' he said. When I pushed a bit harder he told me reluctantly that he had grown up in Lakemba in southwestern Sydney and his father, Herbert, worked as a clerk for a time-payment company and lost his job when the Depression hit. Herbert Cook did what thousands of other men did at the time – he left his wife and three children (Ken had a much older sister and brother) and went on the wallaby, looking for whatever work he could find anywhere in Australia. I got the impression that he did this not to help his family so much as to escape from his familial responsibilities. It was very clear to me that Ken had not been particularly fond of his father.

Herbert Cook evidently came back occasionally, but by the time Ken was twelve his father had left the family for good. Ken's sister and brother were now working, so Ken and his mother were on their own. They were close, and Lily Cook did whatever work she could find to scrape a living. 'She sold margarine door to door,' said Ken. 'Horrible white stuff in little cubes. I'd go with her. She'd knock at someone's door and smile and say, "Would you like to try this? I think you'd enjoy it."'

I was beginning to understand why Ken so disliked George Johnston's portrait of the Depression: too many bad memories of his own. Ken and his mother left their house and moved around, looking for the cheapest rent possible. Lily eventually became manager of an inner-Sydney boarding house. 'I'd help after school,' said Ken. 'I had to chase rats out of the kitchen with a broom, and I was also very good at physically evicting drunken prostitutes.' He made this sound like a menial job successfully done – there was that airy tone again – but I believed he was telling me the truth, particularly as he got off the subject as soon as he could. I could tell he had never forgiven his father for deserting his mother and the family, but it was a long time before I discovered the consequences. Though Ken's children knew their grandmother well and loved her, they were told that their grandfather had died years before. Not for many years did they learn that Herbert Warner Cook had lived on into old age. They never met him.

Other clues about Ken's background – and consequent prejudices – gradually emerged. One night we were watching TV on my tiny set in the living room. I can't remember what the program was now, but Ken derisively imitated someone who spoke with a very broad Australian accent. This shocked me a bit. I hadn't considered him snobbish at all, and had assumed that judging someone because of their voice had disappeared years before – possibly about the time the ABC started employing on-air staff with Australian voices instead of pseudo-Brits with carefully rounded vowels. When I protested he told me that when he was a teenager his mother had carefully put aside money for him to have elocution lessons. Lily Cook wanted her youngest child, who was obviously very bright, to succeed in life, and that meant transcending his background, for top people did *not* have strong plebeian accents. This class distinction lingered: I recalled that my own parents, especially my mother, came down on us like a ton of bricks if they caught us using Australian slang or American expressions.

When I was researching *Out of the Bakelite Box*, my book about Australian radio, the actor Leonard Teale told me that one of his first roles was as a stockman in an ABC radio play, and he thought that such a character would come from a working-class background similar to his own. But the producer insisted that he use a sort of unaccented English voice instead, on the grounds that the accent Teale used was 'sloppy'. Most Australian actors of the 1950s could do a huge range of accents, from Russian to Cockney to southern American. The only accent that was unacceptable was a strongly Australian one. (And incidentally, anyone who thinks this kind of cultural snobbery has gone the way of the FJ Holden has only to remember the criticism levelled constantly at the voice and accent of former PM Julia Gillard.)

Ken told an endearing story about Lily Cook. When he was a small boy, he said, she would take him to the local lending library. Like other such places dotted around the suburbs of Sydney, this was basically a cubbyhole close to the railway station, run by a local shopkeeper who charged a couple of pence to borrow a book. 'I'd get out a Biggles book,' he said, 'and Mum always asked for "a romance, not too light".' This became a catchphrase of ours.

Ken and his mother, I gathered, remained strongly attached to each other, two people forming an alliance against a hostile world: *contra mundum* was the only Latin phrase I ever heard Ken quote. Having met other charismatic men who were close to their mothers, I have formed a theory. Such men often take for granted that, whatever they do, they will be approved of and loved and accepted, especially by women, and very often they are. Unstinting maternal encouragement, I think, seems to give an extra dose of vitamin B12 to the male ego. For good or ill. But a vein of sadness, like opal in stone, often runs under this assurance in men who have grown up without fathers and who have had to become adults quickly. Ken Cook was one example, Clive James another.

The search for male role models may take young men to strange and difficult places. In the case of Ned Kelly, whose father died when he was twelve and who suddenly had to become the man of the family – he was also the only member of his family who could read and write to a reasonable standard, having almost completed primary school – his father figure and mentor was a criminal outlaw named Harry Power. Ken, with a rocky start in life, was much luckier in his family, and probably brighter too. When he left school at sixteen – he had won a scholarship to Fort Street Boys' High, a very select school, and disappointed his mother by not going to university and perhaps becoming a doctor – he found surrogate fathers in the older journalists whom he met on country papers. When he decided to convert to Catholicism in his early twenties, he was heavily influenced by several priests in country towns, as well as by the family of his wife Patricia, especially her brother. These men, for whom education was important, gave him a taste for reading and discussion. They were very important in drawing Ken towards a career as a writer.

Ken had been more or less staying with me at Bellarion Court for about six weeks when the phone rang early one afternoon. The voice at the other end said, 'It's Megan. Is Dad there?'

Several things about those five words took me

aback. First of all, the caller had given only her name without any other identification, so she obviously assumed I knew who she was. I did, of course: Ken's younger daughter, the second of his four children, a freelance magazine journalist and the child I suspected he was closest to. Megan knew who I was, and some acknowledgement of that would have been welcome, perhaps a sentence beginning, *Hello, Jacqueline, we've never met but …* It would also have been nice if Ken had told me he had given my phone number to his children.

Squashing down my annoyance while wondering what Ken had told his children about me, I handed the phone over to Ken and went on with what I was doing. It was impossible to avoid hearing his side of the conversation, and his responses were widely spaced and monosyllabic: 'Yes, that sounds all right … Well, why not change it to … No? OK, I see. Yes, good.'

When he got off the phone after about fifteen minutes, he explained, 'She's writing a magazine piece. Just wanted to run a few ideas past me.'

I could see why having a father who was a writer could be useful if you were making a career in journalism yourself, but I couldn't help feeling that Megan, now in her early thirties, should have been able to generate her own ideas without having to consult him. Under my high-flown thoughts about writerly responsibility was of course resentment that she had not as much as acknowledged my existence.

When I tried to express some of this to Ken, admittedly without revealing my own feelings in detail, he just looked at me patiently. I didn't understand how the Cook family worked, he said. They were a team. They worked together and always had, ever since the children were old enough to know what a writing career was about. He had made a point of including his kids in everything he did, right from the time they were extras in Patrician Film productions. As teenagers they had spent time at the Butterfly Farm, looking after the animals, driving the toy train around the property, selling sweets and drinks. Kerry had co-authored the novel *The Film-Makers* about the Australian film industry; Megan had illustrated *Play Little Victims*, a satirical book on overpopulation. Paul had written a song to publicise *The Killer Koala*. I already knew that Ken had used the family for material in several of his own books; the children had featured in *Blood Red Roses*, an early comic account of the family's European tour, and *A Letter to the Pope from a Sixteen Year Old Australian School Girl*, a book of Ken's black and white photographs depicting the family's visit to the Vatican, contained a commentary written by the teenage Kerry.

Having all the members of your family working together on common projects and supporting each other's work sounded exciting, even idyllic. I couldn't imagine such a thing in my own family. But wasn't it a bit claustrophobic as well? Ken had dropped, casually, that his youngest son, Anthony, a barrister, didn't live at James Street with the others and wasn't involved in the writing game – 'though he writes very well,' said Ken. What would happen to this tight-knit group, I asked, if they all wanted to live elsewhere or do something else entirely?

Ken laughed at the very idea. He suggested that we should return to the house in James Street, where this time I could meet Kerry and Megan. I agreed – it was good that he felt our relationship was ready to be displayed to his world, and I wanted to see how the Cooks worked together – but I didn't necessarily expect it to be a comfortable experience. Both Kerry and Megan, I knew, were not much younger than I was, and I needed no reminder of the difference in age between Ken and me, eighteen years to be exact. I also had reservations about Megan because of her telephone manner. But I agreed, and a date was set.

When we arrived Ken knocked lightly on Megan's door on the ground floor. No answer. 'She's probably with Kerry, working,' he said, and led the way up the stairs. As I followed a few steps behind, I wondered what we were likely to find. Two women banging away on typewriters opposite each other, a 1980s version of Charlotte and Emily Brontë?

Ken tapped on the door of Kerry's apartment, called 'Hello, possum!' and we went in; it wasn't locked. The living room, dominated by a large TV set with VHS tape cassettes and pillows scattered around, was identical in size and shape to Ken's but much cosier. Brightly coloured plastic toys also indicated the presence of a small child. 'In here!' called a cheerful female voice, and I followed Ken into the adjoining bedroom.

Perched on the double bed were two women in their early thirties and a small girl clutching a pillow. 'Hello.' The slimmer of the two women, propped against the bedhead, nodded coolly at me. She had a classic oval face and brown eyes, with dark hair brushing her shoulders: a barefoot *quattrocento* beauty in jeans and T-shirt. 'I'm Kerry, and this is Sophie.' The little girl at the other end of the bed was a miniature version of her mother, and she gave me a three-year-old's industrial-strength scowl. Megan was shorter and stockier than her sister, with short curly black hair, green eyes and freckles and a straight nose like her father's. While Kerry was lounging, apparently quite relaxed, Megan sat upright; her air of intense suppressed energy reminded me of Ken. Her own hello was polite and cautious.

Ken turned to Sophie and patted his shirt. 'Don't you want to see the wombat?' He explained to me that he and his granddaughter had a game about an invisible wombat that lived in his pocket. 'Remember the song?' He started to sing in an off-key, rumbling baritone: 'Wombats sleep in the daytime, they never sleep at night at all …' But Sophie huddled close to her mother and refused to play.

Ken sprawled across the bed and I perched at the end next to Sophie with my back against the wall. It was not the most comfortable position, but it was good for observation, especially as I turned out to have very little to contribute to their conversation. What struck me most, probably because it was not always my own experience, was the ease and warmth that Ken and his daughters shared with each other. They chatted mostly about their journalistic projects – Kerry and Megan were collaborating on a series of magazine articles about famous historical romances and had started to run out of lovers to write about – and what Paul and Anthony were doing, which appeared to involve a great deal of surfing. Ken was teasing them, and chuckling; behaving, I thought, more like an affable elder brother than a father. I could see that he and Megan had a special rapport, and continued to be fascinated by the physical mannerisms they had in common: the same sardonic arch of the eyebrow, the same thoughtful tilt of the head.

After about three-quarters of an hour my back was really aching, and I was relieved when Ken decided we should go. As we drove down the hill towards the Spit Bridge, I mulled over the meeting. It hadn't been awkward, exactly, just marked by polite indifference towards me. I found this disappointing. I was so fond of Kerry and Megan's father that I had hoped for greater warmth, more of a friendly welcome. But then I reminded myself that I was expecting far too much. For one thing, I had no idea how many women Ken had introduced to them since he separated from their mother, and they had no way of knowing whether or not I was simply another temporary addition to their father's life. I hoped I wouldn't be, but time would tell.

'How do you think that went?' I asked Ken.

'What do you mean?'

'Megan and Kerry. They weren't very friendly, I thought.'

'Weren't they?' He sounded surprised. I was beginning to realise that Ken was not always attuned to nuance in human relationships.

'No,' I said. 'They were not.'

'Give them time,' he said. 'When you get to know each other better you'll get on like a house on fire.' Maybe, but I wasn't inclined to put any money on it. Anyway, I told myself as we drove through Mosman, at least Ken seemed to assume that our relationship wasn't just a temporary, casual thing, which I was happy about. And having seen Ken's easy rapport with his daughters also stopped me worrying about the age difference between us.

Now that Ken's children and I had met, they – Megan and Kerry but seldom Paul or Anthony – resumed almost daily contact with their father. They telephoned frequently, and Ken spent at least one afternoon a week at James Street. I seldom went with him. I wasn't excluded from these meetings, but I saw no real reason to go. As the days and weeks passed, my feelings about Ken's relationship with his kids were still mixed. As for my relationship with them, we would have to spend a great deal of time together for that to change, but they seemed no keener for that to happen than I was.

I was critical of Ken for revealing to me so little about his early life, but as I look back now on our first weeks together I know that in some important respects I wasn't exactly making my life an open book either. In fact, the bright little Clive Jamesian anecdotes I doled out about my childhood in suburban Normanhurst probably came from the same impulse as Ken's yarns: to deflect from certain painful truths and experiences.

For his own understandable reasons, Ken had given me the impression that his parents had never been close and that their marriage had not been successful, partly because of the hardship they faced during the Depression. My parents, on the other hand, had met at the end of the war, a time of optimism and conviction that a better world was on its way. Dad was a dashing young army lieutenant who had won a Military Cross in Borneo, Mum a glamorous blonde secretary at the ABC who had recently been NSW amateur tennis champion. They had had what is known as a whirlwind courtship – six weeks – and married at St Mark's Darling Point, a society church in Sydney's eastern suburbs.

When we were small my sisters and I were convinced that this was exactly how love and marriage ought to work; you found the love of your life and married as soon as you possibly could. And if your parents looked like Clark Gable and Grace Kelly, as we were convinced ours did, what could possibly go wrong?

Mum and Dad and we three girls settled down in a rambling old house in Normanhurst. Dad worked as a personnel manager for various companies. He was a man whose life was coloured by deep respect for commerce and its possibilities and he enjoyed what he did, bringing home trophies such as ashtrays plastered with company logos to prove it. (Robert Drewe's father, as described in his memoir *The Shark Net*, could have been Dad's blood brother.) Mum, like most 1950s wives, stayed at home, looking after my sisters and me.

My mother didn't enjoy domestic life, though (unlike me) she was very quick to learn new practical skills, such as painting walls and making clothes. She wanted to meet people, to use her brain, to work in the world – but the era was against her, and so was her health. She suffered from rheumatic fever when my sister Mardi was little, and her heart was weakened. Like most of her contemporaries she was also a heavy smoker: her standing order at the local corner shop was two packets of Kool cigarettes and a packet of Bex. As she grew older she battled against her lack of physical

energy and purpose, and the warm, loving woman she had been became anxious and, we could see, unhappy.

By the time I was about ten, Mum knew that she had not made the best possible choice of husband. She wanted emotional companionship, but Dad was not someone who knew how to give that. The son of a successful fire-and-brimstone Seventh Day Adventist preacher, the second of eight children with an elder brother and with sisters much further down the pecking order, Dad had grown up with a view of women that owed something to St Paul's. Even though he had a wife and three daughters and he loved us all, he was the first person to admit that he did not understand women or their emotional needs. He had a very limited grasp of the anxieties and the thwarted ambition and expectations that drove my mother, let alone what could be done. His way of handling all this was to spend more time at the office. At least he could control the work he did.

Over time Mum and Dad turned away from each other. Mum eventually took refuge in medication. She believed that if one pill was good, two were better – and her blood pressure tablets and sedatives, which slowed and blurred everything, were best of all. As children we often came home from school to find a stranger in the house, a woman who picked fights with us, who slurred and stumbled, who would take herself off to bed, leaving us to work out what was in the house for dinner. We hardly ever brought friends home.

Being a self-centred adolescent, I did not fully understand what was gnawing at my mother's heart – and nor did I really want to. And then one Saturday afternoon when I was in my early twenties, working as a journalist for the ABC and having recently moved into a rented bedsitter, I went to my parents' place for a visit. The house was silent: Dad was playing golf and my two sisters were out. Mum, I assumed, was in bed asleep. But when I went into the bedroom to check I found her sitting up, with a Penguin paperback on the blanket beside her. I was astonished to see that it was a copy of Betty Friedan's *The Feminine Mystique*, the ground-breaking polemic widely credited with starting off the 1970s feminist movement. Friedan describes 'the problem that has no name', the nebulous but real unhappiness of comfortably-off married women with homes and children who yearn for something more in their lives. I couldn't believe that my mother, of all people, had a copy.

'Read it,' she said, and there were tears in her eyes. 'This is about me. Don't let it be you.'

It was an unforgettable moment. Mum and I did open up to each other more after that, and by the time I left to travel overseas we had reached the stage of going to see movies and having coffee together. She waved me goodbye, smiling, and she did not say what my departure cost her.

That was the last time I saw her. In May 1973, while I was in France, she died of a stroke, in bed, beside my father. She was fifty-one.

I didn't find out for three months, and not until after I called home from Siena. Even then Dad didn't tell me – I gave him my address and he sent me a letter that arrived a week later. I found out that he had told my friends firmly he would let me know about Mum when he judged the time was right. He believed that this was the only overseas trip I would ever have (he had not travelled much himself) and that, as I could do nothing about what had happened, it was best I should stay where I was. In my grief and anger I believed he didn't care about me, he didn't care that his wife had also been my mother, and what I might be feeling. My family hadn't even told me about the funeral, which meant they didn't want me at home, I had no place, I had been cast adrift. Well, if that was how things were, that was fine by me. I didn't need them, I didn't need anybody. It took me years to understand that in his utterly wrong-headed way Dad had done what he thought was best, and longer still before I forgave him.

I stayed in London, vowing never to return to Australia. Then at Easter 1974 I had another letter from Dad. My youngest sister, Avril, aged twenty-one, was dead. Dad gave no details but Mardi told me she had died from an overdose of chloral hydrate, a morphine-based sedative easily available over the counter at the chemist. I tried to tell myself that there was nothing I could do, that – again – it was all too late, and they didn't want me anyway. But I knew that I had to go back.

I spent the time on the 747 to Sydney in sleepless anguish, just thinking about Avril. Six years younger than I, much more volatile temperamentally than either of her sisters, she was always rebellious where Mardi and I were conservative. She had left school as soon as she could and drifted around for a while, trying out drugs, finding boyfriends who turned out to be pretty hopeless. But she was street-smart too. At the age of seventeen she hitchhiked to Wollongong and was picked up by a truckie, and when he moved on her she told him she was going to Wollongong to visit the STD clinic. She got to her destination without any problems. She also had a good singing voice and real flair as a comic actress. About a month before she died I called her from the payphone near my bedsit; we giggled so much that I kept forgetting to put the 20p pieces into the slot and was cut off more than once. But most of the time she was fiercely bored, unable to find a direction for herself. As Mum had done a couple of years earlier, she gradually slipped behind a wall of drugs, spending most of her time asleep. I was sure then, and I am sure now, that she did not mean to kill herself, that her body just gave up. An open finding was recorded, which was a relief to Dad: at least it couldn't be said that his daughter had committed suicide.

Coming back to Sydney, having to face the knowledge that I would never see my mother or sister again, I tried to pick up the threads of a piece of cloth frayed beyond recognition. Mardi and I clung to each other, remembered events from our life together, analysed, tried to make patterns, to understand, as people do. When we turned to Dad for support or tried to encourage him, even beg him, to tell us something of what he was feeling, he refused. He would not discuss Mum or Avril with anybody. All he said to Mardi and me was that we would have to find our own comfort. Then after a while, without telling us where he was going, he packed up his car and left. He went to Queensland, but we did not know exactly where he was for more than a year. Mardi and I had no idea whether he was alive or dead.

We now think he had some kind of breakdown, and the only way he knew to deal with his grief and guilt was to go away and be alone. Opening his heart to his daughters, the people who should have been closest to him, was something he could never do. I understand this a little: it is an impulse I know in myself, the need to go to ground when things are bad, but this did not make it any easier for Mardi and me. Dad hardly mentioned the deaths of his wife and daughter to us, or to anyone, until the day he died.

When I decided to tell Ken what had happened to my family – I can't remember now exactly how the subject came up, just that it did and I felt the time was right – I thought I would be able to explain the whole situation calmly and succinctly. But as soon as I started I knew I couldn't make a story out of this; the words jammed in my throat. All the feelings I thought I had 'dealt with' came to the top in a fearsome tide. I wanted to stop, to tell myself that this was all ancient history, but I had to go on, trying to explain why I had been looking across a desolate, bombed-out landscape where my family had been, and why I was, still.

I can see myself sitting at the kitchen table that day, muttering apologies, my pride in stoicism, in being someone who could handle anything without displaying much emotion, gone. The words were out, I could not snatch them back. *Please don't judge*, I prayed. Ken was silent for a few minutes, just looking at me. He didn't move towards me, he didn't hug me. What he did was hand me a clean cotton handkerchief. 'Cry if you need to, sweetheart,' he said. 'You have things to cry about.'

Nobody had ever said that to me before. What Ken's words did was to make me feel less lonely, to show me that he was in my corner, that he understood. He softened the carapace I had spent so long constructing around my heart. If it is possible to pinpoint a time when you know these things, that was the moment when I fell in love with Ken.

IT'S ONLY MONEY

At Bellarion Court, Ken and I manoeuvred carefully around each other. It was impossible to avoid the fact that we were two large, tall people in a space that seemed to be shrinking by the day. I have always had to fight my tendency to be a pack rat, which I justify with the excuse that you never know when a particular piece of paper or book will come in handy for reference. (Of course when you need the bloody thing you can never find it, but that's a separate issue.) I did not want to admit that this trait may have a genetic basis – Dad was always furious if Mardi or I was rash enough to throw out one of his ancient, yellowing *Sydney Morning Heralds* – so I did try and keep the clutter down. All the same, there were times when my place looked like the post office in Terry Pratchett's *Going Postal*.

Ken would watch me hauling around green garbage bags with some bemusement. As I had observed, he didn't seem to possess much in the way of chattels. I often wondered what he had done with his work materials. Surely after twenty-five years of writing and travelling around Australia he must have a collection of notes and photographs somewhere? However, whatever or wherever they were, he clearly did not consider them to be important enough to be kept with him.

What he did bring from James Street – and what I teased him was his dowry – was a silver picture frame about sixty centimetres long and thirty wide. Mounted on red inside the frame were three telegrams. The smallest, undated, was addressed to 'Mr Ken Cook Coordinating Director Liberal Reform Group'. The text consisted only of the name of the sender: 'President Praesidium South Vietnam National Front Liberation Central Committee'. In the centre was a much bigger telegram, bearing a message in capital letters:

> *THANKS FOR YOUR INTEREST IN VIETNAM PROBLEM STOP USA IS WAGING AGGRESSIVE WAR IN VIETNAM STOP LET USA END ITS AGGRESSION AND WITHDRAW ALL ITS TROOPS AUSTRALIAN TROOPS AND TROOPS OF USA SATELLITES FROM SOUTH VIETNAM COMMA THEN PEACE WILL RETURN IMMEDIATELY STOP GREETINGS HO CHI MINH.*

This was pasted next to a telegram dated 1 December 1966 addressed to Ken and headed 'Commonwealth of Australia Postmaster Generals Department'. This one had a brief message:

> *THE ACCOMPANYING MESSAGE HAS BEEN DELAYED OWING TO AN INSUFFICIENT ADDRESS BEING SUPPLIED BY THE SENDER.*

Ken was immensely proud of these documents, and it was not difficult to see why: there cannot be many Australians who have received a telegram from Ho Chi Minh, the President of the Democratic Republic of Vietnam, especially at a time when Australia was enthusiastically participating in the US effort to destroy him and his country. Ho Chi Minh was probably too busy to work out the proper postage arrangements for Australia, we decided.

This series of telegrams was all that remained of Ken's short-lived political career. He brought nothing else to my place, apart from his clothes, mostly casual trousers, shirts and T-shirts. There was nowhere for them to go except in my wardrobe, which very soon looked as if it was full of people struggling to escape.

Ken himself was almost comically careful not to take up more room than absolutely necessary, and not to interfere with the editorial work I was doing.

He had a project of his own: more short stories for a sequel to *The Killer Koala*, encouraged by his publisher. At first he decamped to the local library, armed with a couple of biros and a school exercise book. After a few days he came back, announcing that he couldn't work there. 'Too many people,' he said. 'They're all old, and they all have hearing aids that squeak. It's like trying to work in a room full of mice.' At my suggestion he took over the living room while I worked at the table in the kitchen. This was a less than ideal use of space; every time we wanted to eat I had to pull papers and dictionaries and reference books off the table and find somewhere to put them on the floor. I should probably add that when Ken moved in we did not go to restaurants nearly as often, and if we did they were not expensive ones or we made do with takeaways. This particular courting phase seemed to be over, and that was a considerable relief.

I was agreeably surprised to see how companionably we managed to live together. For such a large and assertive man, Ken knew how to be invisible; there were times when I would look up and be surprised that he was actually there. We could go for hours without speaking to each other. Though I had lived with men in the past, never before had anyone moved into the space I was used to commanding for myself. But I found it very easy to concentrate on work when Ken was around, largely because he was working too. With Ken, unlike before, I never longed for my own private physical space. It was enough to have it in my head when I needed it. It was also great to be working away busily and find myself engulfed in a hug from a friendly bear who smelled of smoke and lemon. Ken had a habit of stitching kisses on the top of my head, always picking his time to do this at the least romantic moments, such as when I was eating spaghetti or blowing my nose or putting on my bra in the morning. He would also tell me, *I love you, Jacqueline Kent, and I'm very grateful for your existence.*

So, having finally decided that I would go with this relationship wherever it might lead, I was happy. For Ken, I discovered, things were a little more complex. One afternoon he came back from James Street wearing an elegant shirt I had not seen before, dark blue with a narrow white stripe. Kerry and Megan had given it to him as a birthday present a couple of years before, he said, and he hadn't worn it much. When I told him I liked it as a change from his usual casual gear, he didn't look as pleased as I had expected.

'You don't think it's too young for me?' he said. 'You don't think that if I wear it I'll be announcing to the world that I'm an old wreck trying to recapture his youth, because I'm with a bird who's a lot younger than I am? I don't look like a silly old fool?' Even though he spoke lightly I could sense the anxiety behind this. It went with his occasionally calling me 'Foxy' because, he said, I sometimes looked as wary as a fox sniffing the wind and ready to be off any second. I supposed I could understand all this, considering the arithmetic. I was eight years older than his elder daughter. His granddaughter could have been my child.

I looked at this large, crumple-faced man with his greying hair and beard and concerned face and could not find the words to tell him what I knew: that he was my best companion, my lover, the man who made me feel, in the words of Isak Dinesen, *Here I am, where I ought to be.*

Not long afterwards he asked me – in the impudent tone of voice that was his signal that he might be crossing some sort of line – why a *gorgeous bird* like me hadn't been *snapped up* before he came along. 'In other words, why I'm not barefoot, pregnant and in the kitchen?' I replied, which should have given him a few clues about my attitude. Surely he didn't think I was lying to myself, and to him, and that I would soon leave him for someone who would give me what I truly wanted – a baby – before it was too late. But evidently he did. So I told him what I knew to be true: long ago I had decided that a life with my own family was not for me. I cannot say that I was always completely easy about this decision – the force of convention was sometimes strong, and I liked and was interested in children – but I had never felt the visceral need for a child of my own. When I had finished spelling this out, Ken's sceptical expression told me he believed that before too long a sudden rush of hormonal regret would engulf me, that I would become pregnant and demand that he support our child: not something he wanted to do in his late fifties. This was exasperating but there was nothing more I could say.

Then a couple of weeks after that, he sheepishly told me he had visited a local GP and asked whether it was normal for a man of his age to be with a woman who was so much younger. After a few brisk anatomical questions the GP, a man of some sensitivity, smiled and said that if we were both happy, and sex was fine (which it was), there was absolutely no problem, younger women did have relationships with older men, it was certainly not abnormal and Ken was worrying unnecessarily. Ken seemed happier after that, and I noticed with some relief that he gradually stopped talking about gorgeous birds who might secretly be hankering after children.

'You haven't got much jewellery, have you?' he said to me one day. 'That's good for me. I intend to bedizen you.' I wasn't entirely sure that I wanted to be covered in jewellery, though I was naturally charmed by his intention. Ken made a point of stopping and gazing in the window of every jewellery shop we passed and pointing out something he thought I would look wonderful wearing. This was always a delicate filigreed necklace or earrings. When I explained that such intricate, small jewellery would be almost literally lost on me, he looked hurt. 'I always bought jewellery like this for Patricia,' he protested. 'She liked it.'

'She's small and slim with dark hair and eyes, right?' I said. 'Doesn't look a lot like me, then?'

He eventually understood and – with some hesitation – started showing me large plain Swedish pieces, which I did prefer. The promised total bedizenment never really happened, though jewellery-purchasing expeditions became routines that were almost vaudevillian. Ken would announce that I needed new earrings, perhaps, and we would head to a jewellery shop, either in town or on the Corso in Manly, not far from James Street. There we would pore over glass cases while the shop assistant beamed fondly upon us. Once the decision had been made and the item wrapped, Ken would casually wave his hand and say to me, 'Pay the lady.' I would hand over my credit card and sign the slip, fully aware that the salesperson's expression was changing from indulgence to outrage. We would leave the shop with her eyes boring into my back, and I knew what she was thinking: *Paying for your own present! What sort of man have you hooked up with?*

Ken used my credit card – and always reimbursed me – because he did not own one himself. At first I had assumed this was because he disapproved of them, as some people still did during the 1980s, and was being commendably cautious about racking up debt. I soon realised how wrong I was.

A few years before we met, I discovered, Ken had been declared financially bankrupt. When he told me this, in his airy everything's-fine voice, I went into a panic, my mind flashing to *Bleak House* and *Little Dorrit* and *Daily Mirror* photographs from my childhood showing men in handcuffs being led from court by grim-faced cops. Bankruptcy to me meant hopeless grinding bureaucracy, years of court appearances, poverty, drunkenness and several kinds of ruin.

Not so, said Ken – and the story he told me was in many ways emblematic of the 1980s, the time when Australia seemed to float on a glittering tide of cheap money and people with no security borrowed to the hilt. Early in the decade, to encourage the film industry, the Hawke government had changed the *Income Tax Assessment Act* to give a 150 per cent concession to investors in local films and television programs. This section of the Act, known as 10BA, soon became a rort, with people who had no real interest or expertise in making films putting money into movies, many of which were never made.

With a group of like-minded friends Ken invested in a particular film project but for some reason, instead of organising a tax write-off as other investors did, he personally guaranteed the entire enterprise, which meant he would be liable for all debts it incurred, if any. The deal with his partners fell through, the movie was never made and money was owed, he told me. The debt, though substantial by 1980s standards – about $120,000 – was not insurmountable, but Ken could not pay and was declared bankrupt.

This of course was not the whole story, as I found out later, though I still do not know some of the details. Certainly the failure of the movie deal was a contributing factor in his bankruptcy, but it hadn't been the only one. The killer was the demise of the Butterfly Farm, to which he had so casually alluded during our first lunch together. Those two huge floods in successive years had ruined the business, and I guessed that Ken had put his house up as his share of the debt. A couple of shady accountants had not helped matters either.

I wondered why Ken, who prided himself on knowing about money and who had made a fair bit in his time, had allowed himself to get into such a mess; after all, he had been successful in real estate and other deals. There was the bad luck of the Butterfly Farm, of course. But I also came to realise that he had a stubborn faith in the nexus between money and friendship. Because he trusted his fellow investors, who were after all his friends, and because of his firm belief in his own financial acumen, and a certain carelessness, he had not put decent fiscal safeguards in place. For someone so astute about his fellow beings, so inclined to take a jaundiced view of them and their motives, it was quixotic that he believed unquestioningly a man's word was his bond, especially if that man happened to be a friend. Ken was nothing if not a believer in tribal loyalty, implicit and explicit, a stickler for all the clauses of the Old Mates Act. What he saw as his friends' betrayal and failure to help him were more important to him, more irksome and disappointing, than the actual bankruptcy.

However, he told me about the proceedings and their consequences without shame or embarrassment, as if the whole affair was nothing more than a nuisance. The point was, he explained, that being bankrupt did not last forever; normally he should have been discharged after three years. However, at the end of that time he had not been released from bankruptcy. This he put down entirely to the bastardry of his trustees, the representatives of his creditors. They were convinced that he had assets, including large sums of money, that he had failed to declare. Hanging over his head was the trustees' threat to examine him and other witnesses in court to get to the bottom of all this. Until they were satisfied, they refused to discharge him.

I was naturally disposed to be indignant on Ken's behalf. However, I couldn't help noticing that his answers to the trustees' questions – and they kept after him, every few weeks sending severe letters that he picked up from James Street – could be equivocal or too clever by half, and that consequently the trustees increased their efforts against him. I couldn't see why Ken seemed compelled to make his financial life more complicated than it needed to be. But I came to realise that he liked tweaking the noses of his trustees. Annoying them was a game, part of a story he was telling himself, and he enjoyed pushing the plot along. The game was irresistible, the story was the thing, and he also despised his trustees for their piffling obsession with mere money.

I had a dramatic illustration of his attitude to cash when we drove down to Berrima in the Southern Highlands south of Sydney one weekend. It was a cold, dark night, blowing a gale as we walked from the car to the restaurant where we were having dinner. Ken was carrying our cash, about five hundred dollars' worth – and he accidentally dropped it before we got to the restaurant. The notes whirled away on the wind: we never did get any of it back. I was worried; Ken was truly unconcerned.

I never really got up to speed with Ken's financial

affairs, not in detail. Now I wonder whether anybody did, including Ken himself. Of course I was not entirely a stranger to financial complication; I had a few relatives who had carried out dodgy deals of various kinds, including an uncle who my mother firmly believed was half a step ahead of the police. But Ken's combination of insouciance and love of financial detail – he would try out sums in the margins of his exercise books, reminding me of Mozart's manuscript scores with fiscal calculations among the musical notes – was new to me.

For Ken, money formed part of a narrative as compelling as words, maybe even more so: he was extremely interested in how it worked and what could be done with it. My minimal interest in matters financial irritated him, and he accused me of not taking money seriously. This irritated me in turn – of course I took it seriously, never having had much of it – but only in terms he found frustratingly limited. He couldn't believe that in the 1980s he had found a woman whose financial practices, he believed, were about as sophisticated as keeping money in a sock under the mattress.

'Look,' he would say, grabbing a piece of paper and a pen. 'This is how we can make it work. See? If The Company borrows ten thousand dollars and lends it out at eight per cent ...' Scribble, scribble. 'But if we decide to put twelve and a half at eight point five for three years, or maybe at nine for a year and a half ...' Asterisks, ascending and descending arrows, dollar and percentage signs, and numbers marched all over the page. I stumbled along behind, feeling the cloth-headed panic I recalled so clearly from primary-school mental arithmetic tests. Ken's hypotheticals always reminded me of those problems that start with the ominous words *If it takes four men ...*

The Company, the entity always invoked in these sessions, was the most important feature of Ken's financial landscape. Like other bankrupts, Ken had no existence as an independent fiscal entity, though he was allowed to work, and did. All the money he earned from royalties and journalism went into The Company, of which his children were directors and he was technically an employee. I came to look upon The Company as a large and formidable machine with levers, wheels and arms that could be pushed and pulled depending on the result required, like some of those apparently benign but menacing contraptions of Bruce Petty or Shaun Tan. I was reconciled to the existence of The Company except for one thing. It meant being more closely involved with Ken's children.

Kerry, Megan, Paul and Anthony had very little if anything to do with our day-to-day fiscal matters; they did not contribute to The Company and their role was effectively to sign documents or make out cheques.

The chief signatories were Kerry and Megan, and I sometimes wondered whether they enjoyed having to be so closely involved with their father's financial affairs. Kerry had family responsibilities of her own and Megan was busily earning her own living as a freelance journalist. But Ken, who had clearly trained his children to be financially literate, certainly much more so than I was, had the habit of discussing his money with them at length, although I noticed that they very seldom if ever offered advice.

It was all very well for Ken to have a warm, friendly relationship with his children, and I still envied that. However, I couldn't help resenting the way he intruded them on our affairs. But so it was, and clearly he wasn't going to change. He often talked about gathering the people he cared about behind a six-foot-high wall, where they would be protected and safe: *contra mundum* again. It was a very attractive, even wonderful, idea and he meant it absolutely. But I sometimes thought that he would build this protective wall only if he found the bricks and mortar, and worked out by himself what the wall should look like, and constructed it to his specifications and no one else's.

DOWRIES

Whenever I thought about what I had told Ken about my father, I felt a little queasy. I had been as honest about Dad as I knew how to be, but truth can shapeshift so easily. I fretted about whether I had been entirely fair to Dad, whether I had explained him properly. I was also fully aware that I had told Dad almost nothing about Ken. I wasn't sure what they would make of each other when they eventually met, as I knew they had to sometime. And – a minor point – in light of Ken's casual and affectionate acceptance of his own children, how would he react to a father and daughter who habitually greeted each other with formal jocularity and the words, 'Greetings, parent' followed by, 'And the Lord be with you'? *Well*, I thought, *they'll just have to put up with each other, that's all.* At least I was fairly sure they both knew how to behave.

Ken had already met my sister Mardi. The three of us had had a hilarious dinner one evening at a local Chinese restaurant. Mardi had bad laryngitis at the time and couldn't speak, but she hadn't let that keep her out of the conversation. Armed with a biro and several blocks of Post-it notes, she had scribbled replies and comments all through the meal. I think Ken was not quite sure what had hit him, especially when by the end of the evening the entire table, including the lazy susan in the middle, was a blizzard of yellow paper.

Dad and Ken shouldn't meet at Dad's small apartment, I decided. This was basically a bedsit, one room with a small bathroom and tiny kitchen, permeated by the dank smell of old paper: books with curled pages swollen with damp, ancient bills, yellowing copies of *The Sydney Morning Herald*, leaflets presented to him by former colleagues in the Seventh Day Adventist church who occasionally visited and who had evidently not given up on him. Anything Mardi or I put down on a horizontal surface seemed to vanish immediately – examples of camouflage that would have impressed David Attenborough.

I could have suggested that they meet at Bellarion Court. But the addition of a third large person would make the place very small indeed, and I didn't especially want to advertise the fact that Ken was living there with me. Dad's views about cohabitation without marriage were very clear. Besides, I knew Dad would insist on driving himself to my place rather than taking the train. This was not a good idea. His eyesight was not what it had been, nor were his reserves of patience.

Like a lot of retired older people Dad spent a great deal of time alone, listening to and watching the ABC and writing indignant letters to *The Sydney Morning Herald*, which declined to publish them. He was a great reader, usually about the history of World War II, or biographies of famous men. He also had enormous respect for the *Herald*, considering it the Antipodean version of *The Times* of London, a paper that – in its pre-Murdoch incarnation – he admiringly referred to as 'the Thunderer'. A staunch follower of the *Herald*'s conservative political line, he basically believed that the Liberal Party knew what they were doing and must be allowed to continue doing it. He and I were at daggers drawn about political issues; Mardi, who was less interested in such things, tended to placate him. But it was she who once commented that Dad recognised two points of view. One was his, the other was wrong.

Dad and I did find common cause in our shared enjoyment of words and pithy phrases. I always appreciated Dad's particular way of expressing himself. When I was in London he sent me a letter that ended, 'Well, the stamp says PREVENT BUSH FIRES, so I must go and do that.' And towards the end of his life, a reluctant convert to word processing technology, he picked up a computer floppy disk and said to me thoughtfully, 'Did you know, beaut, this thing holds enough words to fill Sydney Harbour seven times?' Once he described a shady lawyer he knew as 'a man who takes up a position on the far edge of the law and faces inwards'. (That's one of my favourite lines of his. It came forcibly to mind years later, when I was editing and writing books about Australian politics and some of its practitioners.)

Given Dad's early life in a rambunctious Seventh Day Adventist family, with his father a preacher, it is not surprising that the King James version of the Bible and the *Book of Common Prayer* were part of his linguistic DNA. Like his parents and brothers and sisters, he was completely unselfconscious about using ecclesiastical phrases in ordinary conversation: 'Well, I told this bloke, there's no health in you!' When besieged by worrisome people he would growl, 'Lord, how they do increase that trouble me.' (Useful, that one.) He would send up the cadences of the *Book of Common Prayer*: 'So I said unto him with one accord ...' I know that once you have grown up with these things, they tend to stay with you. One of the reasons I enjoyed Jeanette Winterson's brilliant novel *Oranges Are Not the Only Fruit* was that it brought back so much of the fundamentalist Christian language I knew as a child.

And in Manning Clark's *History of Australia* I could hear the rhythms of my grandfather's speech. (Clark's father had been a minister of religion, too.)

Dad's love of sonorous phrases was reflected in his fondness for particular authors; the plays of Wilde and Shaw and books by Thornton Wilder were what he called his 'top shelf' books. He very seldom read fiction, and I think this stemmed from his childhood, when novels had been considered frivolous. Possibly because of this he tended to view makers of art – musicians, artists, writers – with suspicion. I believe he thought there was something unmanly about a bloke who spent his working life holding a paintbrush at an easel or sitting at a desk writing.

So putting together my father and Kenneth Cook, the author of many novels and a converted Catholic – and therefore belonging to a church widely regarded by Adventists of Dad's generation as the Antichrist – was not to be undertaken lightly. What would they talk about? Work history was a non-starter: before his retirement Dad had held many jobs, working for a range of private companies, mostly in sales or personnel management. Ken had left school before completing his secondary education; Dad had degrees in classics and economics. Politics? Ken and I were basically ALP supporters; during the 1961 credit squeeze Dad had looked into the abyss and *almost* voted

Labor. He was keen on golf and rugby union while Ken would not have known one end of a club from the other and basically regarded rugby as a prison riot with a football attached. Dad was interested in history; Ken, as I already knew, disliked looking backwards in any way, including historical events. Shared knowledge and understanding of the bush? No in italics.

In the end I decided that Ken and I would take Dad to lunch at a restaurant of his choice. He nominated a steak restaurant not far from where he lived, about forty minutes from Bellarion Court by car and close to the train station at Pennant Hills, a northwestern suburb of Sydney.

That Saturday turned out to be one of the last warm days of the year; the light outside was so bright that when I stepped into the restaurant I could see nothing. After a moment or two of afterimage I looked around for Dad. He was sitting right at the back facing the door: Wild Bill Hickok guarding against ambush in the Deadwood saloon.

He had not chosen the most cheerful venue for this epic meeting. Small tables dotted throughout the room were each lit by a candle in a blood-red globe, and a strong smell of barbecued flesh came from the kitchen at the back. Above us was a beaten copper engraving that showed a matador about to slaughter an innocent horned beast. The place was a shrine to the glory of meat.

Dad rose to his feet as we approached. I was touched to see that he had made an effort: he had had a haircut and he wore a red and grey long-sleeved Viyella shirt I hadn't seen before and grey trousers that I suspected had once been part of a business suit. He greeted me with, 'G'day, beaut,' followed by a hug and three firm pats on the back.

Seeing him and Ken together I realised what a big man Dad still was. In his prime he had been six feet four tall and broad with it. Now, in his late sixties and a martyr to a bad back, he was a couple of inches shorter than that and stoop-shouldered. I had not seen him for some time, and probably because I was there with Ken I looked at him with new eyes. I was struck by how white his hair now was, making his blue eyes seem even bluer, and how stiffly he moved, as if hewn from a block of wood. Increasing age sometimes pares back a face towards androgyny, but Dad, with his round face and snub nose, looked like an ageing boy. Ken, though almost as tall, was much less solidly built. In jeans and a short-sleeved green shirt, his curly hair and beard trimmed, he looked rather like a lecturer in the humanities department of a small university.

They shook hands firmly and we all sat down. As I had expected, conversation failed to flow. As the three of us made sporadic remarks over our glistening steaks and coleslaw, as we sipped the raw red wine, I was faced by an awful fact, one I had not really considered: the only subject Dad and Ken had in common, the one that for obvious reasons they could not discuss, was me.

And so we struggled through the meal. Then almost at the end Ken said to Dad, 'I believe you won a Military Cross during the war.' His tone was deferential. Dad gave him a long, level glance. 'Yep,' he said. 'I opened a tin of bully beef and there it was.' *Oh God*, I thought, *I hope he's not going to be rude, I hope he's not about to tell Ken it's none of his damn business.*

Dad had never told my sisters and me exactly why he had been awarded that crown-embossed silver cross attached to a white and purple ribbon, and he had always changed the subject if any of us asked. However, we knew that it was one of our three sacred objects from The War. Another was Dad's army jacket, which lived with his good business suits and shirts and ties and which emerged from my parents' wardrobe three times a year, when we had our birthday parties. On the evening before a party my sisters and I would help Mum put sweets into small white paper bags that she carefully tacked all over the front, back and sleeves of Dad's jacket. The following afternoon we would wait in the yard with our guests for the moment when Dad, rustling all over and apparently covered with miniature sandbags, appeared in the backyard and invited us all to chase him. He would run and dodge skilfully around the back lawn and the flame tree, pursued by a bunch of shrieking little girls intent on grabbing as many lollies as possible.

The third object was a wicked-bladed samurai sword in a white scabbard covered with black spidery characters. This was the first really foreign object I ever saw, and when I was very small I would climb up to the top of my parents' wardrobe to look at it, though never to touch. Was that dark stain blood? Had Dad taken the sword from an enemy soldier he killed in hand-to-hand combat? He never said. I thought it was strange that he had kept this trophy, because we knew exactly what Dad thought about the Japanese: they were brave but treacherous, and we could easily have been living under their domination. Dad didn't like to be reminded of them in any way. For one thing, we were forbidden to wear rubber thongs or flipflops. The official parental line was that these were bad for our feet, but we knew that Dad hated looking at shoes that resembled those the Japanese had worn in the jungle. And when I bought a secondhand Toyota Corolla, Dad was very reluctant to ride in it – and I doubt that this was entirely because of my driving.

'Please tell me how you got your MC,' said Ken to Dad. I could see Dad thinking over whether he would tell the story or not. After all, he hadn't told his own daughter about this, and Ken was a man he had just met. But he took a deep breath and, to my surprise, he began.

When I look back on what followed, I think he wanted me to know more about this time in his life, about the young man and soldier he had been, but had been unable to tell me directly because the masculine subject of war was unsuitable for discussion with young daughters; he would certainly find it easier to talk about with another man in my presence. Possibly, also, there was an element of one-upmanship in describing his role in a war that Ken had been too young to fight in.

Dad's words came slowly at first, but as the memories crowded in he spoke more rapidly and with greater animation. In mid-1945, he said, as the Pacific War was limping towards its end, there was mopping up to be done in the islands north of Australia. Accordingly Lieutenant Lance Kent, aged twenty-eight, found himself and his platoon of thirty-seven men on a beach close to Balikpapan on the island of Borneo, with orders to storm into the hinterland and take Japanese positions. There were only two problems: he discovered that his map was inaccurate – he might have been given the wrong one – and his walkie-talkie did not work.

With no idea where the enemy were or how numerous they might be, and unable to radio his base for further orders, he told his men to move about a mile inland along an escarpment to its highest point, from which they could reconnoitre. On the way up, the platoon found the entrance to a tunnel dug into the hill. Dad knew that the Japanese used these tunnels as strongholds and storage rooms and ordered one of his men to use his flamethrower. A huge scarlet blast was followed by a few minutes of silence. And then, from inside the tunnel, a dreadful sweetish stench rolled towards Dad and his men.

'Human flesh, roasting,' said Dad nonchalantly. 'Ever smelled it?'

'Ah, no,' said Ken. His eyes held the predatory gleam of the writer who is being given information. 'What's it like?'

'They tell you it's like barbecued pork,' said Dad. 'They're right.'

The platoon continued their climb, reached the top of the escarpment and dug in as fast as they could. It was close to midday and hot, getting hotter, and they had no idea how long they would have to stay there. And then at about a quarter past four in the afternoon they saw a number of Japanese soldiers charging up the rise towards them. At the same time, a group of Australian soldiers on patrol were approaching from the side, forcing back some of the enemy. Dad had to think fast. The question was whether he had enough men to reinforce the Australian patrol as well as hold the higher ground against the enemy. The risk of being exposed was worth taking, he decided. He and about a dozen of his men ran down the ridge towards the other skirmish, picked off the stragglers and returned to their position. Then, as darkness fell, they waited for the remaining Japanese to strike.

Dad said that that night was among the worst of his life. He and his men had no idea, still, how many of the enemy were near them. But they couldn't move, and as time passed they grew increasingly hungry. Above all, they did not know how long their water would last. And so they waited, knowing that the most likely time for an attack was the hour before first light. But dawn came, then morning, noon, and still nothing. Then, two hours before darkness fell, Dad and his men heard heavy machine gun fire from the side of the ridge closest to the sea.

Australian soldiers! And members of their own battalion, too. The platoon was saved, and Dad had lost only two men in the skirmish with the Japanese. Several hours later, during kit inspection back at headquarters, Dad found that his men had been so disciplined that none had run out of water. As their leader, he said, that made him even prouder than the medal he was awarded. The level of trust between him and his men as well as their discipline were what mattered most to him that day.

Dad's story was long in the telling, and we left the Pennant Hills steakhouse in the late afternoon. Ken was uncharacteristically quiet. He and Dad shook hands, he thanked Dad for telling him the story; Dad, perhaps feeling that he had given away too much, brushed his thanks aside almost brusquely. Neither made any plans to meet again.

'He's great, your dad,' said Ken as we drove down Pennant Hills Road towards the city and Bellarion Court. Relieved that the meeting had gone better than I had expected, I thought about what I had just witnessed. Here were two men born in the same country twelve years apart, separated not just by time and life experience but by their attitudes to war. Dad, from a pacifist background, had nevertheless signed up to defend his country and remained a firm supporter of Australia's involvement in the Vietnam War; Ken, who had opposed that war, had done what he could to prevent his sons fighting in it. Yet because of Dad's war experience, they had achieved some kind of rapprochement, however temporary.

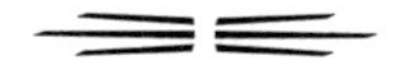

Ken and I had been together for several months now. We must have looked as happy as we felt: strangers smiled at us in the street. In the evenings at home I sometimes watched him as he read the paper or a novel, his face serious with concentration behind his old smeared glasses, and joy surged as I thought, *I really love you.*

Like most couples we had set habits, which we recognised in each other. Ken was an unabashed carnivore, liking nothing better than to hoe into a well-done steak, accompanied by potatoes, or other vegetables if I insisted, which I did. I liked salads; he disdainfully picked at them, regarding them as fit only for rabbits and ungulates. He couldn't bear anything remotely resembling a crispbread: if God had meant man to eat cardboard, he said, he wouldn't have invented bread. He followed the Bloke Diet, in other words, and I did my best to make sure it was reasonably healthy. 'I'll erode your standards,' Ken would tell me, eyes gleaming.

Ken was an enthusiastic smoker and drinker, and his eager embrace of alcohol never wavered. Most of the literary people I knew drank more than was good for them, and so did I. But Ken's consumption was often heroic: he described himself cheerfully as 'a lay alcoholic'. He frequently started off the day with a beer after breakfast, followed by the best part of a bottle of wine at lunch and another at dinner. Late in the evening was his time for a few slugs of 100 Pipers whisky. As far as I could see, however much he drank his behaviour did not change at all. He never slurred or repeated his words, he was generally amiable, even when he felt like having an argument, and unlike many dedicated drinkers he was never tedious to listen to.

He knew, of course he did, that prolonged drinking was not the best thing he could do for his health, but any doctor with the temerity to suggest he give it up would have been laughed to scorn. Ken truly believed that drinking made him a better writer; he declared that he never trusted writers who didn't drink. And he would certainly have agreed with Kingsley Amis that 'no pleasure is worth giving up for the sake of two extra years in a geriatric home'.

I cannot say I sat back and watched him: rather the reverse, there were times when I matched him glass for glass. Sometimes I felt as if I was playing Lillian Hellman to his Dashiell Hammett, until I realised that I was putting on an alarming amount of weight and decided to pull back. But I never gave up drinking with him, because I enjoyed it. At the same time alcohol per se was never as important to me as it was to Ken. I believe now, as I did at the time, that he could not have done without it, or cigarettes either. Now I know I should have tried harder to reduce his consumption of both – but I cherished our late-night whisky conversations, was in love with Ken as he was, and really didn't want to play nursemaid.

We didn't become hermits by any means. We saw friends for dinner, usually only one or two at a time, basically because my Sylvia Plath stove wouldn't cope with any more. I had become rather preoccupied with the changes in my life during the past few months – Ken did have a way of taking up a lot of time – but when I finally introduced him to my women friends they seemed to enjoy meeting him, and he enjoyed them.

He did set them tests, however. The most common one involved their attitude to abortion. Most of my friends, like me, were generally relaxed about the subject. Ken, on the other hand, was anything but. How, he asked passionately, could abortion ever be justified?

The first time he broached the subject I was perplexed: I had thought that because our political views aligned, we agreed on other important things. Was I standing on the edge of a generation gap, or was this simply an element of Ken's adult conversion to Catholicism? Most of my women friends took his views in good part and argued their corner with equal passion. Ken, though strongly argumentative, was never aggressive; he usually backed down if his opponent scored a valid point.

A frequent visitor to our place was Brian Davies – one of the few people, Ken used to tell me, he could steal horses with. Brian, who was a lovely bloke, sometimes looked at Ken with a kind of quizzical and affectionate resignation, an expression I later saw on the faces of some of Ken's other friends. Their bond was deep and enduring: they had been through a lot together. When I first met Brian, he and Ken had jointly leased a small motorboat moored near Manly. Ken was never happier, I think, than when roaring across Sydney Harbour, our wake unzipping behind us.

Ken was always concerned about other people's illnesses and operations. This surprised me, probably because I was in fairly rude health myself and was accustomed to not paying much attention to illness, my own or other people's. *Don't cry or you'll have something to cry for* was the approach to sickness that I had grown up with, hearing family legends about people like my father's Uncle Harry, whose leg had been cut off in some awful agricultural accident and who ripped up his shirt to make a tourniquet, chucked the leg in his friend's ute, went to hospital and recovered splendidly. But when, for example, a close friend of mine needed to have her shoulder restructured, Ken remembered exactly where and when and at which hospital, and called her several times. He could also be very aware of people's needs. A friend's fourteen-year-old daughter had an intense desire for a pet. Her father did not see this, but Ken did. 'I think we should buy that girl a puppy,' he said, 'so she can love something of her own.' He didn't get around to that, unfortunately. This anxiety about other people was an unexpected feature of his character, and it made me love him all the more.

When it came to his own health – even though he had had a very close brush with mortality the year before we met – he was cavalier to say the least. If his daughter Megan, an avid reader of the *Monthly Index of Medical Specialities*, suggested he should look after himself better he would reply haughtily that he was fine, as healthy as a mallee bull thank you, in that airy tone that was nevertheless so implacable. He always carried with him a cheap brown briefcase containing not just the exercise book and biro he used for work, but half a bottle of 100 Pipers whisky, two packets of

Ransom cigarettes, and blister packs of Tenormin and Minipress for his angina and blood pressure.

All he had to do was eat well and exercise moderately, he told me, and all would be fine. He and I were reasonably conscientious about both, often going on long walks together. Any form of more organised exercise he considered ridiculous: whenever we passed the local gym he would snicker loudly at the sight of twenty women scampering around to loud music. He had cheated death, he was going to kick fate in the balls. In his view mild exercise and a good diet would cancel out the effects of nicotine and alcohol – and he made it as clear as could be that nothing was going to change his mind.

DOING YOUR DARG

Looking back, I find it surprising how much literary work Ken and I managed to do. This was, of course, mostly out of financial necessity: of the two of us I was the one with the more regular income, which was ironic considering that freelancing as an editor has never produced anything like a dependable pay cheque. I kept doing it because I liked it. The Novel was now a set of notes in a cardboard folder and I was content for it to stay there. I never talked to Ken about my own writing ambitions – time enough for that, I thought, when I had produced something I was really proud of. I rather wished Ken would get started on another novel of his own, and once or twice well-meaning people asked whether he had a new book in the pipeline. He always shrugged and smiled, repeating his conviction that 'a novel just happens to you'. Clearly one wasn't happening. He seemed perfectly content to continue writing his bush stories.

Ken's and my rhythm of work were completely different. I have always depended on habit, going to the desk every morning at the same time, being a nine-to-five kind of working person. Ken on the other hand spent a large part of the day appearing to do absolutely nothing – he would sit in the front room staring at the sea, or drink beer in the kitchen and smoke and stare into space, or go for a long and solitary walk. After a while he would grab a fountain pen and scribble a couple of stories in his exercise book, and once he started he kept at work for hours.

When he had finished a story or decided he didn't need to do any more he would stop and announce, 'I've done my darg.' This was an expression I had not heard before, and he explained that it was a Scottish word referring to the number of sheep that shearers were supposed to shear every day. (The word comes from the Middle English 'daywork', I discovered.)

Ken's apparent casualness was the result of having been in the writing game for thirty years. He made writing look easy, didn't agonise too much about choice of words. He was after a good story clearly told. If the reader didn't care what was going to happen next, he said, it didn't matter how pretty the words were. He was always impatient with 'fine writing' for its own sake; in his mind that was another way of saying that *nothing happened*. I am sure he would have endorsed the words of the English scriptwriter and novelist William Nicholson: 'The kind of novelist who thinks that story is a dirty word had better be a genius.'

Getting the story right was something Ken took very seriously, and this applied to the short stories as well as the novels he had written. He once showed me how he worked out a plot, graphing the action in a line from a low base to halfway up the page, dipping slightly then going higher, retreating again before reaching its highest point. This, he explained, was how the structure should be: here the climax at the top, here hold back, move the action further forward here and there, dip to make the reader anticipate a conclusion, finish on a high. He told me this was the way he had always set out his novels' development. I had never seen anybody else do this, and thought this was unique to Ken. I later learned that when Kurt Vonnegut was a writing teacher, he used a similar method to show how story worked. I now recognise that this approach is pretty close to the three-act structure widely used by teachers of writing for film or television.

Ken might not have had a novel he needed to write, but he was always looking for stories or inventing them. It was an ingrained habit. Often in the evenings, over whisky, I would join him. The game we played had simple rules. One of us would say something like, 'What if a tall woman with a club foot came through that door, holding a gun?' The other would add to that, and so it would go on. The chief rule was that neither of us was allowed to say that any plot development was silly: an alternative that would work better had to be invented. Nothing came of these games in a practical sense, but the exercise was fun. Ken told me he used to play similar games with his children when they were young. This was, I realised, the genesis of the Cook family word factory.

There were times when Ken's attitude to his craft puzzled me. One evening he and I went to the celebrations for the centenary of Angus and Robertson at the Sydney Opera House. Everyone connected with Australian publishing seemed to be there. I had a great time catching up with the publishers, fellow editors and authors I knew, and over reasonably good champagne and canapés. Ken of course had a large circle of acquaintances, though he and I didn't necessarily know the same people. As I watched him meet and greet I expected a certain amount of dear-boy, hail-fellow-well-met from him, but – as at Clare's dinner party – he was almost diffident, even monosyllabic, when talking to them. *Well*, I thought, *bankruptcy and illness took him out of the writing scene for a while, and I know he's no fan of large gatherings.* But then Barry Oakley, a successful novelist and playwright and about the same age as Ken, asked him what he was working on. To my surprise Ken suddenly launched into a speech that to me sounded pre-prepared.

'I have never understood why people take so long to write novels,' he said. 'Six weeks is enough for anybody.' I was familiar with his impatience regarding the sort of writer who, in the words of Oscar Wilde, spent all morning putting a comma in and all afternoon taking it out again, but I was pretty sure this was a tease on Ken's part. I didn't want him to carry on like a Great Man of Australian Literature – plenty of others in the room were trying out for that particular role – but I couldn't see why he needed to imply that he took the business of writing so lightly.

But later that evening a bumptious young critic bowled up to Ken and oozed condescension all over him, congratulating him on *Wake in Fright* as a great adventure story. All Ken had had to do, it seemed, was to go out into the bush, look at a few locals, think of a good plot, then flex his fingers and start work, and very soon a completed novel shot out of his typewriter. Nothing to it. Normally the most amiable of men, Ken glared at this young idiot. Clearly it was all right for him to joke about his work, but nobody else was allowed to. 'I'm sure you're right,' he said with the most offensive intonation he could manage – and he could be pretty offensive – and stalked off.

The casual, careless attitude he expressed about

writing did not always fool people. He told me that once, as a writer in residence at the University of New England, while giving what he thought was a cool, reasonable talk about his work and storytelling to some students he became more and more intense. 'I suppose I'm fairly emotional about this, really,' he said. He was startled when everybody in the room burst into understanding laughter.

One thing that surprised and annoyed me was his attitude towards writers' grants: he was dead against them. His attitude wasn't what you could call consistent, since he'd certainly received his fair share of money from the Australia Council. When I pointed this out he shrugged and said that, like prizes, these things are obviously good if you win them. But I can still see him taking small irritated puffs from his cigarette as he listened to my arguments in favour of grants: that Australia's literary culture was small and needed to be cultivated, that grants depended on a fair and expert system of peer review, that buying time to write was crucial for writers who had demonstrable talent but needed to find their voice. He just didn't like the idea, he said – jabbing the air with his crooked middle finger – that Australian writing might be skewed towards writers who received literary grants but produced the kind of work that nobody much wanted to read. If writers were any good, he argued, their work would find an audience, regardless of any government, or other, support. I could see that some of his opposition came from a belief in the school of hard knocks, but I did think his blasé attitude was annoying. Why shouldn't life be easier for younger writers than for his own contemporaries?

He also had it in for 'filthy poets', asserting that they had only to write down a couple of hundred nice words every now and again, and then go to lunch. No problems with plot or character or suspense or any of the other features of what he considered good storytelling. But I found it frustrating that he was so uninterested in the Australian novelists who followed him, the ones I knew and admired, in my generation – Helen Garner, Kate Grenville, Robert Drewe, Tim Winton – as well as older though newly discovered women writers such as Jessica Anderson, Olga Masters and Elizabeth Jolley. In Ken's eyes these writers (not that he'd read them) didn't care about plot or character, but rather what he called 'word decoration'. What had happened to writing for entertainment? he wanted to know. Why was everybody expected to be reverent about Writing? One new and contemporary writer he liked was the crime novelist Peter Corris. Ken admired his character Cliff Hardy, and liked Corris's handling of his plots and his economical use of words. But he didn't praise any of the others.

Shortly after the Opera House party the *Killer Koala* short story collection was ready to be released, and Margaret Gee wanted Ken to go on the road to promote it. Margaret, who was highly efficient and businesslike, was pulling out all stops. She had lined up the major radio, television and newspaper outlets in the country for interviews and had booked flights to the mainland capital cities. Knowing from my years in publishing how much skill and hard work are involved in putting together a publicity tour and, in pre-internet and email days, how many hours had to be spent on the telephone, I greatly admired what she was doing. Knowing less about the mechanics, Ken was not admiring so much as grateful. After his run of bad health and the prolonged stress of matters associated with his bankruptcy, Margaret's faith in him meant a great deal. And while Ken disparaged *the writing game*, I could tell that he was delighted to be back in it.

Margaret had promoted *The Killer Koala* as yarns from a rough-hewn outback storyteller. She supplied Ken with a Driza-Bone raincoat and an Akubra hat and told him to wear them whenever he went for any interviews or public appearances. As I watched Ken absorbing this news, I could see his face displaying what some novelists have described as warring emotions. Sure, he would do whatever was necessary to earn a quid, but did he, a senior Australian writer of some standing, *really* need to get dressed up in this outfit? 'I've never owned a Driza-Bone or one of those hats,' he said plaintively, only to be told briskly that now was his chance. It was only Ken's unwavering trust and affection for Margaret that made him accept these conditions, but he did, with reasonably good grace.

A couple of days before the tour was due to start – and he insisted I come with him, which Margaret very generously agreed to, paying also for my airfares – he thought he might as well get into the spirit of the thing. 'Look at this,' he said. 'I got it years ago; it's been in a cupboard in James Street.' *This* was a stockwhip, a proper one with a plaited leather handle. It looked very dangerous, and I told him so.

'Not if you know how to use it,' he said. He told me that the trick was to flick your wrist downwards quickly. 'I'll show you.'

We were standing in the living room of Bellarion Court. 'No, don't, not here—' I said. Taking absolutely no notice, Ken held out the stockwhip at arm's length and jerked it sharply downwards. The tip flicked up and the large Japanese lampshade exploded in a mess of paper and wire.

'Thanks, Clancy,' I said. We left the stockwhip at home.

One of my cherished memories is of Ken at Sydney

airport ready for the first leg of the tour, glowering under the brim of a too-small Akubra perched on top of his head, swathed in a brown oilskin raincoat that smelled of candle wax and clutching the biggest toy koala I have ever seen, pressed upon him by Margaret. When we got to Melbourne, we waited for our luggage at the same time as two kids, a boy and a girl, aged about six. Their eyes widened in delight when they saw the Killer Koala sailing forth on the carousel. Then Ken, attired in his bushman costume, stepped forward, snatched it and stalked off. As I followed him I glanced behind, and the expression of contemptuous envy on the faces of those children will ever remain with me. The Killer Koala made only that one trip; next time we left it behind to be hugged by Ken's granddaughter Sophie, who was roughly the same size.

Once Ken got into his stride on the publicity tour his professionalism came to the fore and the props were forgotten. I watched him being interviewed by a range of newspaper, television and radio journalists in five states, and he was never less than engaging and funny. He told the story of the killer koala at least fifty times, and he made it fresh every time. (I've only once heard another Australian author manage that kind of spontaneous candour, and that was another pro. When *Schindler's Ark* came out Tom Keneally answered the inevitable 'how did you come to write it' question many, many times – and as if he had never heard it before.) What made Ken's interviews work so well, I think, was the contrast between his solemn face and cultured voice and the ridiculous stories he was telling. Interviewers and audiences loved him and Ken enjoyed every minute of it as far as I could judge. He was in his element: telling stories, making people laugh.

On the last leg of the tour we went to Perth, where the local branch of the Australian Society of Authors invited us to afternoon tea. The Society's doyenne, fondly fussed over by other members, was Mary Durack, then in her seventies. In her rose-pink dress with white cardigan and pearls, her grey hair elegantly swept up into a French roll, she looked ladylike and sweet.

Someone fluttered up to her and said, 'Here's Ken Cook, dear, he wants to meet you,' and Mary Durack made the usual goodness-me-you've-come-all-this-way remarks. Ken asked her about *Kings in Grass Castles*, her classic account of her pioneering family establishing its pastoral empire in the nineteenth century, and a book I knew he admired greatly. Immediately her eyes grew sharper and she entirely dropped her little-old-lady persona. With assurance and authority she spoke about the outback Australia she had always known in her bones and, for about fifteen minutes, the two writers talked about the world they had chosen to describe. They understood each other perfectly. As we left Ken said to me, 'She's great.' And then almost to himself he added, 'There's a woman who really knows her country.'

BE IT EVER SO HUMBLE

The Killer Koala sold something like 30,000 copies – excellent sales, then as now. An invigorated and newly confident Ken settled back into life in Bellarion Court. He spent a lot of his time preparing more yarns for a follow-up book to be titled *Wombat Revenge*, and maybe a third one in due course, while I went back to editing.

After the round of hotels, radio and TV studios, flights and taxis, it was good to resume familiar domestic patterns. I recall that part of our time together in a succession of small snapshots: long, laughter-filled arguments (one of his most reliable teases was to declare that Jane Austen was no better a writer than Georgette Heyer, who wrote more interesting stories anyway); visits from friends; companionable drinking; Ken and I reading after dinner, him wearing the crooked, sticky-tape-mended glasses he refused to replace; walks around Lavender Bay and down to the ferry wharf and further afield around Manly; sorties onto the harbour in the motorboat. And under it all, sustaining everything, was the ground bass, the ostinato of our life together, a steady beat of love and affection. For the first and probably only time in my life I lived wholly in the present, suspended between past and future.

So I was caught flat-footed one afternoon in late September 1986 when Ken came home from visiting James Street and announced, 'We need to move out of here.'

He had never as much as hinted that he was dissatisfied with our living arrangements. 'We've lived here long enough,' he said. 'It's time we moved.'

Something about the way he said this, as well as the words themselves, put me instantly on guard. He looked charged up and rather pleased with himself. Knowing his history, I suspected this might have had something to do with a deal of some kind. And so I enquired, with just a touch of trepidation, whether he was making a general statement or had some plan in mind.

'I've found us something to buy,' he said.

I think I had expected a discussion about renting a bigger place, nothing like such a sudden decision. It was financially impossible, surely he must have known that. His much-vaunted expertise as a purchaser of real estate had let him down, I thought.

'We can't afford to buy anything,' I pointed out.

He shook his head irritably, as if a fly had buzzed too close to his face. He had been talking to an estate agent in Manly, he said, and this man had encouraged him to think about buying an apartment opposite Queenscliff beach. This was a really good buy, he said. We would pay only the interest on the asking price for two years and we, that is The Company, could easily afford that.

'And after two years?' I asked.

'We can sell the place if we want to,' he said, as if he was explaining the ten times table to a rather dim child. 'We should get onto this now. The deal won't last. I've got the papers here.'

I was silent, fighting hurt and outrage. How could he even think of doing this without consulting me? This wasn't the way we were supposed to work! We were a team, together, *contra mundum*, weren't we? How *dared* he go ahead and make this decision? And did he really think I would greet this mad idea with enthusiasm, having sprung it on me like this?

Taking my speechless state for agreement, Ken started painting an idyllic picture of what he imagined as our new home. The apartment he had found had two big bedrooms and a large living room and was practically on the beach. We could get up as late as we liked in the morning and stroll across the road for a plunge in the surf, then saunter down to Manly shops ten minutes away for an early lunch of fish and chips, before strolling back to the apartment and perhaps doing a little writing. In the evenings after dinner we would walk along the beach, watching the moon rise over the waves ...

'Let me think about this,' I said.

Ken snorted. 'What's to think about?'

Well, quite a lot, for me. Queenscliff was the suburb next door to Manly, and Manly was where Ken's children and his wife Patricia lived. If we moved there I would certainly see Ken's children more often, we would have more to do with each other, and being pulled further into the Cook orbit was absolutely not what I wanted. I quite liked Kerry, Megan, Paul and Anthony, whom I was coming to know better. They were pleasant, though our association was governed solely by our various connections to Ken. If not for that, I thought, we would probably never have met, for we had little else in common, certainly not cultural references or life experiences. I had no children so I could not make common cause with Kerry, the mother of Sophie; Megan, potentially the one with whom a friendship might develop over time – I had come to enjoy her sense of humour, so like her father's, and the biting wit that was exclusively her own – was still a little prickly and cautious around me. Paul and Anthony were never less than amiable, but their passion for surfing I knew nothing about, nor could we talk about rock or pop or folk music. By inclination and training I was firmly wedded to the printed word. The world of Ken's children, who were about a decade younger than I, had been dominated by film and television, and we had few if any books to talk about or to share. Though we had all grown up in Sydney, our backgrounds, our childhoods, had been very different, I thought.

As far as I was concerned, Ken's children were quite involved enough in our lives already, as the shareholders and directors of The Company. Even though they had very little to do with the day-to-day running of the thing, and even though I too was now a director though not a shareholder, the fact remained: Ken's children and I were now legally linked, and I was not keen on that.

More important to me, however, was the place of Bellarion Court in my own life. That little rented apartment, shabby though I knew it was, had been my working world – and my home. After moving in and out of various apartments, I felt stable and happy there, and I thought Ken had understood that. He had been invited to share it, and the decision had been mine. I felt, however irrationally, that if I agreed to move away from Bellarion Court on his terms I would be losing control over my life.

Ken finally realised what my reaction actually meant. 'Look, I know this isn't something you were prepared for,' he said. 'But I want you to have something lasting out of our relationship. I want you to have a place of your own for when I'm no longer here. Something that's yours.'

'But I haven't even seen the place,' I said.

'Doesn't matter. We need to decide. Now.' His mouth was set, his eyes hard. The man standing in front of me was someone I did not recognise. I did not like him. And so I dug in.

'Don't talk to me like that,' I said.

'Oh, all right,' he grumbled. 'But you have no idea how much I hate having to explain things to women.'

I drew breath, then told him exactly what I thought about that comment, and with a vehemence and intensity that I think surprised us both. I normally hate conflict – will go to some lengths to avoid it, in fact – but not in this case. This seemed like a fight we needed to have, and one where a lot was at stake, certainly for me. This fight felt like a struggle for my own autonomy, for my own sense of self. I thought he had understood and accepted me as an independent woman. To find that in his mind we were not equal, that he was telling me that things had to happen his way, and he was only consulting me over this because he had to – that felt like a betrayal of what, from the beginning, I had assumed our relationship to be.

The row that followed – it was too complex and heated to be classed as a simple disagreement – lasted for several days. Meeting opposition he had not expected, Ken adopted a superior I-know-best tone that simply added fuel to my fire. I was never a match for him in argument: whenever I become really upset about something words tend to jam in my head, but I stood my ground. All through that weekend and beyond, while we alternated between snarkiness and icy courtesy, I found myself thinking about Ken and Patricia, what their marriage might have been like. Had he always carried on like this if he failed to get his own way? Did he *ever* think about other people when it came to something he wanted, especially if it involved money? For the first time I understood a little more about something that had always puzzled me: why Patricia, even with four children, had walked out on Ken. If this was how he always behaved when challenged, I thought, marriage to him must have been intolerable.

After a number of thoroughly unpleasant days Ken and I reached some kind of truce, not least because neither of us enjoyed fighting much. I agreed to check out the apartment; he agreed that nothing more would happen about the financial arrangements until or unless I said I was satisfied with it.

As a result I did some investigation of my own,

and was pleasantly surprised. The terms he had been offered were certainly sustainable for us. Property prices in Sydney were rapidly going up and showed no sign of faltering, so restructuring the mortgage or selling the place in two years' time was reasonable. And I had to admit that the thought of having a place of our own, a home we both liked, was attractive. I didn't tell Ken any of this – after the last few days I wasn't about to admit I was softening my attitude in any way – but I was prepared to think again about the issue. And so, in the spirit of one who is making an enormous concession, I took myself off to look at the apartment.

It was one of four in a white-painted building directly opposite the beach at Queenscliff, so close that wisps of sand drifted across the narrow road that followed the shore. The building was separated from the footpath by a white picket fence, and the apartment had a flat-fronted picture window and a tiny balcony. It stood out as the first tarted-up building on the block; surrounding it were shabby wooden bungalows, formerly boarding houses, recalling a time just after World War II when farming families fled the parched western plains and came to the seaside for the Christmas school holidays.

The apartment was painted white and carpeted, with windows down the side and rooms leading into each other rather like an old-fashioned railway carriage.

I liked its feeling of light and space, and also the quiet. If you stood still and listened, you could hear the *shush, shush* of the sea. I thought of the tottering piles of books at Bellarion Court versus room for bookcases in the living room, weighed up the large modern kitchen against the primitive Early Kooka stove, noted the wardrobe space in the bedroom and the view from the front room with the sky meeting the ocean, the horizon of blazing blue and infinite possibility. I considered the proximity of Ken's children, decided that I could live with that. *All right*, I said to myself. *Let's do it*.

Telling Ken that I had changed my mind was galling, but I had sound reasons for it, which he had the grace to accept without comment. (I don't know whether I had expected smugness, but I was grateful not to have to endure it.) I wonder now, as I wondered then, whether he really ever understood why I had pushed back at him like that. As I had observed long before, he wasn't a man finely attuned to the nuances of human behaviour, and now I knew the consequences if he was contradicted. But in a surprisingly short time, considering the upheaval, we settled back into our familiar and harmonious routine. We made arrangements for moving house, carefully consulting each other about such things as furniture, what should be kept, what thrown out, what we needed to buy, and we never referred to the fight again.

As we made our plans, I realised that I was happy we were actually setting up house together. But the fight had emphasised one thing for me: once again it made me realise that my long-ago decision not to have a child had been the right one – even though I had been repeatedly told that I would change my mind *if I met the right person*. That was Ken of course, and I didn't want to be with anyone else, ever – but I knew it was much, much better for us to go on as we were.

I still felt a little sad about leaving Bellarion Court, but any regrets dwindled once we had moved into the new place. Ken commandeered the front room, spreading out his papers on a desk he bought, and spent a lot of time gazing at the horizon between writing his bush stories. Acting on some kind of Calvinist impulse, I chose to make my office in the only room of the apartment that lacked a clear view or sound of the sea. Arranging my books in the living room was a particular pleasure. Other women may rejoice in well-equipped kitchens or beautifully arranged linen cupboards; for me the pinnacle of housekeeping achievement is a properly organised bookshelf.

In some ways, living at Queenscliff was like a perpetual holiday. Sustained and concentrated thought was apt to dissolve in the warm, salty air, helped by the knowledge that we could always plunge into the surf if work became stressful or difficult. The only shop near us was an open-all-hours place that sold cigarettes, fried food and ice cream; for anything more substantial we had to go to the shops at Manly. We never saw office workers or schoolkids; sometimes in the late afternoon I would sit reading in the front room while the surfers paddled through the waves opposite and joggers pounded along the seafront. It was difficult to believe that we were living in a serious place.

Ken made at least one highly satisfying discovery about the new apartment: it was perfect for his Pirate King routine. One of his favourite movies, I knew, was the 1983 version of the Gilbert and Sullivan comic opera *The Pirates of Penzance* starring Linda Ronstadt, and featuring Kevin Kline as the Pirate King. Ken loved him. He cackled merrily as he watched Kline, resplendent in billowing white shirt, thigh-high boots and tight trousers, buckling and swashing his way through the plot, always getting his Errol Flynn timing slightly wrong. Ken would watch him on tape over and over again. There were times when I looked up from eating breakfast to behold Ken, stark naked from the shower and with a manic gleam in his eye, stomping through the living room towards me, doing Kline-like moves with a toothbrush cutlass held between his teeth, humming some version of 'With Cat-like Tread'. This always made me choke on my muesli.

The new place also unleashed Ken's desire to be

a singer. I now discovered that he was inordinately fond of Irish folk-songs, every single one of which, it seemed to me, began with something like, 'Oh have you heard the fearful news' and went on to describe in gruesome detail the demise of many children, mass death by shipwreck or asphyxiation in a collapsed mine. I pleaded with him to shut up, and when he asked why (in injured tones) I had to tell him the brutal truth: though he had a beautiful speaking voice, he couldn't carry a tune in a bucket. At this point he became all huffy and I-would-have-you-know about his track record as a musician, informing me that he was a full member of the Australasian Performing Rights Association. This had happened because, during the folk-song boom of the 1960s and 1970s, he had spent quite a lot of time inventing new words for old Irish tunes, recorded by the singer Lionel Long. Ken's musical play, *Stockade*, based on the Eureka Stockade confrontation of 1854 and which I had never seen, had sixteen traditional Irish, Welsh and American ballads, all with new words he had written. He occasionally received requests to put it on: he told me proudly that it had a large cast, mostly of women, so it was popular with amateur theatre and music groups.

Ken didn't know much about the classical music I enjoyed, but he said he liked opera. He didn't know a great deal about that either, but he knew what he liked, and what he liked were set-piece arias, the more emotionally strenuous the better. At the top of this list was '*E lucevan le stelle*' from Puccini's *Tosca*. He never tired of listening to the hero, beautifully and at some length, bidding the world farewell before being blasted by a firing squad. Placido Domingo's rendition was a particular favourite. 'Listen to the sob in his voice!' Ken would say with doleful relish. 'No good without that, is it. Gotta have that sob.'

Late one morning I walked into the kitchen and saw Ken writing at the table instead of at his usual perch, the desk in the front room. He looked agitated.

'Patricia,' he said. 'She's walking past.'

Curious, I went into the front room. Striding alongside the joggers and bicyclists on the beach side of the road was a small, square-shouldered woman with dark hair. In her slacks and sandshoes and T-shirt she looked pleasant, neat, ordinary. So she was the reason why we never bought our groceries at the supermarket nearest us because it was close to Patricia's apartment and we might see her in the tinned food aisle? This was the woman who had made Ken scuttle to the back of the apartment like a guilty schoolboy? 'She doesn't know where we live,' he said when I returned. It sounded as if he wanted to reassure himself, not me.

I knew that the subject of Ken's marriage to Patricia was one of the biggest 'here be dragons' sections of his personal cartography. All he had told me was that after more than twenty years of marriage his wife, who had given up her career as a librarian at the University of Sydney for marriage and children, had been offered a job in the library of the United Nations and announced that she was moving to New York. She had asked her children to come with her, but they were settled in school and university, and so she went by herself to the USA, where she stayed for several years. The marriage was over from the moment she left Sydney.

Ken told me he had no idea why she had made this decision. Knowing quite a lot about his history by now, I could guess. The person who sets up a financial rollercoaster ride and invites other people along may be fun to be with, and you may love him, and the ride itself may be adventurous and exhilarating – but there are reasons, not least long-standing familial responsibilities, why someone who has spent much of the time in the passenger seat might come to find it less than satisfying. And as I discovered later, the failure of the Butterfly Farm – and the sale of their house to pay off Ken's debt as a result – would certainly have contributed to Patricia's decision.

I gradually came to realise that Patricia's departure was one of the most distressing things that ever happened to Ken. He truly believed, I think, that he had created the perfect family, and according to Brian

Davies and others, for a long time the Cook family unit, with everybody pitching in and reasonable discussion about everything, was the envy of many of their friends. When Patricia, with whom he had created all this, no longer wanted to be part of it, Ken turned more than ever to Kerry, Megan, Paul and Anthony. From the time Patricia left he ceased to dedicate his books 'to Patricia' and replaced this with 'to Pam K', his children's initials.

I never really understood why, if Ken was so anxious to avoid his estranged wife, he had wanted to live so close to her. I could only assume that he needed to be closer to his children and wanted to see Sophie grow up, and assumed that Patricia could be easily avoided. I had some sympathy for Kerry and Megan about this: negotiating divided loyalties is never easy. They rarely mentioned their mother to Ken, and obviously said nothing to me. Ken, I knew, never visited James Street at a time when he was likely to see Patricia, and presumably the same was true for her.

Ken wanted so much for everything to be all right – even though he was in large part the reason it wasn't. And being so thoroughly involved in his children's lives showed me that he wanted – perhaps more than almost anything else – to retain the camaraderie and the easy communication the family had enjoyed when they were young, in the glory days when, as Ken once said, 'we were the Cooks'.

But he could not always keep the dragons at bay. Sometimes I would wake up in the early hours of the morning and realise that I was alone in our bed. I would try and get back to sleep, but the expanse of sheet beside me stretched out cold as a tundra. After a while I would get up and head towards the light in the kitchen. I knew what I would find: Ken hunched, fully clothed, at the kitchen table in a haze of cigarette smoke, the ashtray full and a half-empty bottle of 100 Pipers whisky at his elbow.

When I told him to come back to bed, he would say he wouldn't be long and pour himself another slug of whisky. I then had to decide to sit up with him or go back to bed by myself, though he always made it clear whether he wanted my company or not. His abstracted smile was always the giveaway, my cue to leave him alone. I would try and reassure him, kiss the top of his head and tell him I loved him, but his reply was always, 'Do you, sweetheart? There's a pet.' Sometimes he could be as remote and untouchable as that seam of colour in the opal stone.

And so I would return to the bedroom and lie awake in the dark and worry. I would think about those long columns of figures in his exercise books, jumbled up with the short stories he had been drafting, the figures that reminded me of the most unpleasant fact about our life together – that Ken was still in bankruptcy. His trustees, representing his creditors, had never really gone away, and they underlined their presence by sending unpleasant, even threatening, letters. To deal with them Ken had employed a young solicitor, all blond hair and smooth words. I never liked or trusted this man, and I was not sure how effective he was: Ken would come home from their conferences looking just a little greyer than before. There were many nights when I watched the shadows on the ceiling of the bedroom, wondering whether we would ever escape from all this. I wanted to trust Ken's assurances that everything would work out, but I could not quite see how that could happen. Then I would turn over and try to get to sleep.

TRY ANYTHING ONCE

Scene: My office in the second bedroom of our Manly apartment, late October 1986. Books, papers everywhere on desk and floor, coupled with ominous crunching noises from abandoned writing instruments whenever I push back my chair. I am sitting at the desk facing the blank wall, editing the manuscript in front of me. I swear, not necessarily under my breath, as I read for the fourth time an easily-looked-up date error, followed by a glaring mistake in grammar and the blithe contradiction of a point made several pages earlier. Not for the first time I wonder why on earth people want to write books when they can't be bothered reading.

Enter Ken.

'I think we should get married,' he said.

For the second time in two months I stared at him, speechless.

'Ah,' he said, not in the least fazed. 'I see the

problem. I'm not romantic enough for you. You want me to go down on one knee and propose.'

'You'd never get up again,' I told him.

'No, I'm serious. I want us to make a public statement that we're together,' he said.

'I don't see why we need to,' I said. And that was the crux of it, for me. What was the point of demonstrating anything to other people? Didn't he think it was enough to be ourselves, just living together?

He was smart enough to drop the subject while I mulled it over. Knowing him reasonably well by now, I thought I could see where he was coming from. He was almost twenty years older than I, and socially conservative in many ways; maybe he thought it was not right to live with a woman outside marriage. However, a day or two later he inadvertently let drop another reason. Kerry had told her father, 'I think you should marry Jacqueline publicly and with ceremony.' Ken told me this as an indicator that his children approved of our relationship: 'See, darling, they accept you, they want you to be part of the family.' *Well, maybe*, I thought. I didn't have the heart to tell him that, nice though this would have been to think so, I didn't believe that was the main reason for Kerry's comment. More likely Patricia – who couldn't have been pleased that Ken had moved back to Manly with me – had been giving James Street a hard time. The message, I was sure, was more:

If you're ever going to legalise things with Jacqueline, for God's sake do it quickly so we can all move on.

I had never seriously considered marrying anyone, but I was now in love as never before. If marriage was so important to Ken, I supposed I didn't have any really serious objection to it.

'You'd have to divorce Patricia,' I said.

'Of course.' But I saw him hesitate for a moment and thought, *Yes, there's the rub.* Deep down, or perhaps not so deep down, Ken couldn't quite get away from his belief – as a Catholic convert – that marriage is a sacrament ordained by God and indissoluble. I believed Ken when he said he wanted to marry me. I also believed that if he could have done so without divorcing Patricia, he would have.

'We could have a civil ceremony,' he said. 'Come on. Won't hurt a bit. Foxy.'

He hadn't called me that since our very early days together. Did he still believe, as he had said then, that I was ready to leave at a moment's notice? Had he suggested marriage because he believed that this ceremony would be some kind of insurance that I would stay with him? Surely not.

I had come to see that under the carapace of ramshackle, flippant bonhomie he presented to the world, and though in some respects he was one of the toughest people I had ever met, Kenneth Cook was stubbornly romantic. He had endured bad health, a broken marriage, crippling financial setbacks – and now he wanted to turn the page, to write a new chapter in his life. Marrying me would be a declaration of faith in the future, a declaration that life and joy and optimism could be renewed. And because I knew these things, I could not say no.

'So you will marry me?' he said.

'Yes,' I said. 'I will.'

I declined Ken's offer of an engagement ring – diamond solitaires, the whole idea of *being engaged* belonged to a starry-eyed twenty-one-year-old, not to a woman who was pushing forty. But I was so happy – despite recalling the consternation that had greeted Clare's engagement to Ken all that time ago – that I expected our announcement to be greeted with a conventional chorus of congratulation. How wrong I was. Several of Ken's friends and associates, mostly those who had been party to his less successful financial endeavours, were nothing short of appalled. One old friend of Ken's was extremely frank. 'He's old and buggered,' he said. 'Why are you marrying him?' On the defensive I turned flippant, though what I told him was true: Ken was more fun to be with than anyone I had ever known. He looked at me for a long moment. 'Yes, he is,' he said. 'But it's high-cost fun.'

Several of Ken's women friends – and now I

discovered that since his separation from Patricia his amatory history had been fairly extensive – were none too pleased either. (Clare herself made no comment.) More than one of Ken's previous flames thought that if he was going to marry anyone, it should have been her. One woman in particular, who had known him for many years, who had copy-typed his manuscripts and given him emotional support when he was at his lowest ebb, was particularly upset, and she made her feelings known with some force. 'Don't marry her, Cookie,' she told him. 'There's bad blood in that family. Her mother and sister committed suicide and her father's an alcoholic.' (She had been talking to a former ABC colleague whom I had previously considered to be a friend.) From hints I picked up over the following weeks, Ken's children also had to endure a range of opinion and comment from friends of the family.

Dad and my sister Mardi took the announcement in their stride – I think Dad was relieved that Ken was making an honest woman of me at last – but though most of my friends expressed their delight, one or two were less than supportive. A long-term colleague, another editor, raised a satiric eyebrow. 'Editor marrying author,' she said. 'Bit of a cliché, isn't it?' And one or two whom I had counted as friends told me, more or less, that when I had given the matter due consideration I would change my mind. I presumed this advice came from Ken's reputation as a hellraiser, but I couldn't be bothered disagreeing. One close friend whom I had known since our days at the ABC, a woman who disliked Ken, was particularly scathing. We had a row, and unfortunately our friendship never really recovered.

So things were sticky enough. And then one afternoon Ken, who had been to lunch with a couple of old mates, came home looking grim. It took a while for me to winkle the reason out of him, but he eventually said, 'They think you've used your feminine wiles to trap me into marriage because you want to have a baby before you're too old.'

I suppose I should have expected this assumption from somewhere, but nevertheless it came as a shock. God knew I had never been immune to the charms and temptations of gossip, but now I was on the receiving end. I didn't like it much, and neither did Ken. However, instead of voicing his fury at length – as I did – he just shrugged. '*Contra mundum*,' he said. 'Don't ever worry about what other people say, love. Screw 'em all, save six and keep them as pallbearers.'

Ken now had to sever his legal connection with Patricia. For a while he made absolutely no moves in that direction, and – having made a pact with myself not to mention this to him or to anyone else, since it was not my decision – I said nothing. This was not easy.

Having made the decision to marry him I kept wanting to ask, *Well, when?*

It was with this question unresolved that Ken and I left Sydney for a trip to the far south coast of New South Wales, to spend time with old and dear friends of mine. After two weeks of beautiful crisp days and large meals in a comfortable old house, slightly tempered by bushwalking, we left to return to Sydney much refreshed. As we drove through the small town of Eden, Ken suddenly pulled up outside a shopfront in the main street. 'This'll do. Won't be long,' he said, and got out of the Honda Civic. Only then did I notice the word 'solicitor' on the plate-glass window. After about three-quarters of an hour he emerged with an expression of sombre satisfaction. 'All sorted out,' he told me. 'Perfectly straightforward business, divorce. Just a matter of writing letters and waiting.' With that he started the car and we drove off.

I could tell that he expected to be congratulated on his decisiveness, but despite my previous impatience I couldn't bring myself to do it. Patricia Cook, I realised, was about to receive a letter from a country solicitor she had never heard of, telling her she was about to be divorced. Certainly there is no pleasant way of ending any deep and long-lasting relationship, but I did, and do, think Ken could have managed things with greater delicacy. 'Don't you think you should at least tell Patricia directly?' I asked.

'We haven't spoken for years,' he said. 'It'll be fine. Very easy and quick.'

It turned out, of course, to be neither. Weeks passed. Ken grew increasingly fretful. Having done nothing after ten years of separation from his wife, he now wanted the whole business sorted out immediately. There were long and acrimonious phone calls to Eden, and Ken said unkind things about country towns and lawyers who lived in them. As far as I could see, none of this made any difference to the solicitor, his operational manual evidently being *Bleak House*. And Ken never did say anything directly to Patricia, leaving that side of things to Kerry and Megan. They cannot have thanked him for this.

Using our pay-the-lady shopping rules, Ken and I bought me a gold wedding ring. It had a pocked, uneven surface, like a nugget. Ken insisted on engraving our initials inside, together with his motto, and now mine, *contra mundum*. The ring lived in a mole-coloured leather bag that I kept behind a picture in the living room of our apartment. When Ken was not around I would sometimes take it out and look at it, thinking, *This is mine, I'm actually going to wear this.* It was a thought I kept trying on, attempting to get used to it. I felt as I had as a child with a new coat: happy to have it, but unsure about how it would look and feel.

Then one day the divorce papers did turn up, were duly signed, and Ken breathed a sigh of relief. Now he could devote himself to being enthusiastic about the actual ceremony. 'I think we should be married at sea,' he declared. 'Ships' captains can perform marriages, can't they? I shall enquire.' Two hours and many phone calls later he returned, exasperated. When he told the maritime authorities what he wanted to do, they subdued him with an enormous number of forms that had to be filled in, also threatening us with having to meet several people wearing uniforms. Not a romantic bone in their bodies, clearly. So that was that.

Both of us had a horror of sentimentality and, despite what Kerry had said, we didn't want to marry with pomp or ceremony. Ken, I think, was afraid that, despite my refusal about the engagement ring, because this was the first time I had been married I would suddenly break into 'I enjoy being a girl' and demand tulle and lace and orange blossom. (I later thought I should have tried this on just to tease him, but it didn't occur to me.) Though we never discussed this, the truth was that we were both just a little embarrassed at the thought of standing up in public and announcing that we loved each other.

And so we decided on a very small ceremony with only fourteen guests – Ken's family, Mardi and Dad, and a few friends – followed by lunch. Ken wanted to have both ceremony and lunch in the garden of the Stationmaster's Cottage, where we had had our first memorable meal together. I was happy with that, though I felt bad about the size of the guest list. Kent family weddings usually have complete sets of second cousins, and I had old friends I would have liked to be there … but we had to keep costs down.

Now all we needed was someone to marry us. Obviously a minister was out, which meant finding a celebrant. Determined to be businesslike about this, we looked in the Yellow Pages. We chose a woman who lived a couple of beach suburbs from our apartment.

The reason we selected her was that her advertisement, unlike the others, was free of twirly writing, cherubs, small chirpy birds and rosebuds, and we duly made an appointment to see her.

When we walked into her house I felt a strong sense of betrayal, for her home was a Temple of Love. She showed us into a living room bristling with pink hearts, lace doilies, figurines of doting couples in eighteenth-century costume and photographs of small winsome animals. The celebrant, however, was tall, angular and sharp-featured, with permed brown hair and huge glasses, and she smelled strongly of Shalimar perfume.

She didn't gush over us exactly, but she made it clear that she would be quite happy to do so if we gave her any encouragement at all. But Ken and I answered her questions crisply and efficiently, like travellers applying for a joint visa to a foreign country. This obviously mystified her. Few couples who came to her for their love to be sanctified by the state can have demonstrated such a spirit of let's-do-this-and-get-it-over-with.

Her lips compressed, she handed me what looked like a Bible owned by a large and very devout family. 'Here are some readings you might like,' she said. 'You could say some of these words aloud to each other, or ask one of your guests to read.' Inside were a large number of poems and vows of varying length and complexity, each neatly typed and encased in plastic. Obediently I flipped through. Marriage of true love admitting no impediments? A bit tactless given Ken's family history and the agonisingly protracted business of the divorce. *Sonnets from the Portuguese*? Lovely, but perhaps a little overdone. And as for the 'Desiderata', I could just imagine Ken's reaction when told to go *placidly amid the noise and haste* because he was a *child of the universe*. Rhymed promises to be always there for each other, to be each other's best friend? Hallmark card stuff.

I was just about to close the book when I caught sight of a poem with the first line 'My heart is like a singing bird'. It was 'A Birthday' by the Victorian-era poet Christina Rossetti, and I vaguely remembered studying it at school and thinking it was rather soppy. Curious about how much of it I still recalled, I read over the gaudy pre-Raphaelite imagery of pomegranates, doves and peacocks. Nicer than I remembered, but still a bit overwrought. Then I came to the last lines:

Because the birthday of my life
Is come, my love is come to me.

My eyes filled with tears and for a moment or two I couldn't speak. Yes. *Yes.* But I knew I could not possibly say those words in public without breaking down, and I did not want to be so exposed. Nor did I want anyone else to say them. I had learned, as most of us inevitably do, that words often flatten when spoken aloud, their glow will almost certainly disappear. And so I decided to keep those lines for myself. I closed the book and handed it back to the celebrant. 'No, I couldn't find anything,' I said.

In the end we decided upon the basic I-take-you-to-be-my-lawful vows, nothing more. The celebrant wrote the words down and ran us briefly through our legal responsibilities for the last time. We shook hands, her fingers as glacial as her manner, and she said goodbye in the tone of Julius Caesar's ghost announcing that he would be seen at Philippi.

Tuesday 6 January 1987 was one of those blue and gold high-summer Sydney days; the ocean opposite the apartment sparkled with promise. As we breakfasted and dressed, Ken and I hardly spoke. Now the time had come, I think we were both more nervous than we were prepared to admit to each other. I was worried about what I had chosen to wear. I had tried to steer a course between frilly meringue and corporate suit without complete success, and the blue and white dress with pleated skirt and white shoes now struck me as more suitable for a cocktail party than a wedding. Ken, who did not possess a suit, had decided on grey trousers, a dark blue jacket and a dress shirt with a large, flat collar that would have been perfect for the fencing scene in *Hamlet*.

We drove to the restaurant in Ken's battered red Honda Civic. It still smelled rather plaintively of sodden dog and I saluted George the Alsatian, who had been found a good home when Ken moved in with me. We got out and greeted our guests, who were chatting in the restaurant garden. Suddenly I felt very happy. This was going to be a good day.

Everybody was smiling except the celebrant. In her bag with the documents I noticed a biro with an enormous plastic feather quill, the sort of thing used by writers in bad historical movies; clearly this was her last-ditch attempt to impose a sense of ceremonial colour on the signing of the register, at least. Resplendent in maroon and cream, she stepped in front of the tree she had chosen for the ceremony, opened her wedding book and cleared her throat.

Ken walked towards me and stretched out his right hand, the one with the crooked middle finger. 'Come here, woman, and marry me,' he said.

NARROMINE

Early February. We had been married a month and summer was winding down. Along Manly's Corso the shops were starting to pack up their swimming costumes, replacing them with displays of wetsuits and flippers. The summer surfers waxed their boards and put them away, swapping their surf gear for business suits or school uniforms.

Manly was changing. One of the places we loved, the garish funfair at Manly Pier with its red and yellow octopus ride, ferris wheel and seductive smell of deep fried food, was turning into a heap of rusty junk smothered in industrial tape, signalling its approaching metamorphosis into a bland glistening high-rise. I was particularly sad at the demise of the whack-a-mole, remembering a hilarious afternoon when, with a dear friend, we bashed away at randomly appearing metallic moles with a yellow rubber thong. It was impossible to walk anywhere along the waterfront without being ambushed by the rumble and crash of bulldozers, the stutter of pneumatic drills, or roaring trucks. I felt sad that this raffish, careless part of Sydney, this creature of salt and sand that all through my childhood had advertised itself as 'a thousand miles from care', was beginning to exist only in old black and white photographs featured in the foyers of sleek new apartment buildings.

And then it was March, with the afternoon light dropping, the return of the currawongs and the sea air taking on the sting of early autumn. The year was shifting, settling, and we felt it too. Our various workloads had dipped – Ken had nearly finished his third book of bush short stories and my editing work, though constant, was not especially demanding. Even Ken's trustees in bankruptcy had temporarily retreated; we had had no letters demanding money with menaces for quite a while. The trustees hadn't gone away, we knew that, but I was grateful for the respite, however long it lasted.

Without a writing project of his own or something immediate to worry about (or pretend to ignore), Ken was restless. He spent a lot of time at James Street with Kerry and Megan or wandered around the apartment humming tunelessly, stopping at the door of my office for little chats every now and again and driving me mad. Remembering one of my Seventh Day Adventist grandmother's favourite sayings that Satan always finds work for idle hands to do, I suggested that he might like to take up a hobby, maybe building model aeroplanes or collecting stamps – anything to get him out of my hair. I was joking, sort of, and he looked at me reproachfully – he shared my low opinion of any pursuit involving balsa wood and/or glue – but he didn't stop wandering or humming. I was well aware that, however often Ken declared his need for domestic tranquillity and however much he loved the life we had, he was intensely and inveterately restless. For him, routine for too long led to boredom – and he was not a man who tolerated that in any form.

And then one morning he told me he wanted to get on the road again.

I shouldn't have been surprised, really, considering his history. And I could tell he was talking about more than quick trips to southern New South Wales or the southern tablelands or even the Blue Mountains. *On the road* meant a long road trip, duration and destination indefinite. I waited for him to say he had a great idea for a novel and it needed to be researched, but he did not. 'We'll just take off,' he said. 'We'll get a campervan. Just think where we can go! I want you to see so much, the sunsets of western Queensland, the deserts of the Red Centre. I want you to dip a toe in the Arafura Sea ...'

He was aglow with enthusiasm, the whole idea clearly delighted him, and he spoke with a passion I had not seen in him for a long time.

I could not share his anticipated joy with the same intensity. Though I too loved parts of Australia outside the cities, for me these were always on the coast. As for the deep interior, I had hardly travelled in it, but my gut feeling had always been that it was an alien, indifferent landscape. If there had been a continent-wide earthquake, if Australia had twitched its pelt and eliminated all settlement since white people came, it would not have made any difference, I believed, to the feeling or the spirit of the country, especially the inland. When I mentioned my feelings to Ken he scoffed, and I understood why: he needed and wanted to get into the bush, to lose himself in the flat haze, to let his imagination run, to explore his sense of possibility.

But I wanted to discover the man who had understood and shared Mary Durack's love and knowledge of the country, the man who knew how to conjure the bush through his words. Like Ken, I too wanted to escape the whole bankruptcy business, not just because it was always there – and I knew Ken was more worried about it than he ever admitted – but because of its effect on our life together. I badly wanted Ken and me to build up a store of memories, to have experiences that only we could share, to build a history of our own. And so I squashed down my misgivings – our mutual lack of bushcraft skills was part of them too – and agreed that yes, this would certainly be a fine adventure.

Ken immediately flew into action, exhibiting planning skills I had never known he possessed. He organised a tenant for the apartment while we were away, leased a jaunty yellow campervan, decided on a route that ensured we could be contacted at least every couple of days, arranged for work he could do on the road. All this, to my surprise, happened very smoothly. And on a sunny day in mid-April we climbed into our campervan and turned its nose westwards. We headed for the Great Western Highway with Kerry's sardonic last words echoing in my ears: 'Enjoy the motels.'

On the first night we stayed in Blackheath, at the top of the Blue Mountains range. It wasn't a motel, but a bed and breakfast place. Ken said we should test the campervan when we were further away from Sydney and there was no alternative accommodation. (I could see how well Kerry knew her father.) The next morning we got up early and went for a walk before breakfast, following a narrow track that dived down into a purple-shadowed gully. It wound past stands of mountain ash and skirted caves with walls that rippled with all the colours of the earth, from ochre to pale gold and cream. For once I did not mind Ken's shuffling – he had slowed down markedly in our time together – and was content to savour the warm peppery smell of the bush, to trace the patterns of shadow on stone.

As we drove towards Bathurst, gums and dark scrub beside the highway gave way to a straggle of service stations, fast food outlets and car repair places. And now emerged the first real flaw in our travel plan, something that for some reason neither of us had taken into account. In a word: Easter – Easter Saturday, to be exact. Very shortly we were stranded in a sea of metal, car after car around us filled with families or piled with camping gear or bicycles. Half of New South Wales seemed to be on the road and heading in the same direction as we were.

'We'll have to christen the van tonight,' I said to Ken. 'Be proper bush travellers.' He didn't respond and, surprised, I looked at him. He was staring straight ahead, his body tense behind the steering wheel, shoulders hunched, his mouth an almost bitter line. I knew that look, I had seen it when I came upon him in the kitchen late at night. It said *leave me alone* as clearly as if he had spoken the words. But why was he like this now, when we were embarking on new experiences together? Now I came to think of it, he had said very little since we set off from Blackheath, which was odd. Normally while driving he liked to keep a conversation going, to chat about anything that crossed his mind.

But now his whole being seemed concentrated on nothing but the road ahead; now I was sitting next to a grim-faced stranger.

The van continued to crawl towards Dubbo, the sun climbing in a hard blue sky, and my joy in our adventure gradually evaporated. I was bewildered, I had no idea what was happening. Where was the light-hearted ease I had come to know as our common currency, our shared sense of optimism, our laughter? The sense of adventure that had led to this expedition in the first place? I put my right hand, palm upwards, on the upholstered division between the two front seats. This had become our signal for *I love you.* When one of us did this, the other would instantly reach over and clasp the upturned hand: *I love you too.* But Ken did not so much as glance down, and after a few minutes I took my hand away.

It was now well past noon. I was hungry. Breakfast had been toast and a quick cup of tea. 'How about we stop somewhere in Dubbo for lunch?' I suggested.

'No,' said Ken abruptly. 'We'll get something on the run. I want to keep going west.' He still sounded angry. *Well, all right, be like that*, I thought. *But what's the big hurry, for God's sake?* Seething, I said nothing and in silence we headed for the centre of town.

Our progress was slow and hot, and traffic was snarled in all directions. In several places road workers had carefully dug up the bitumen, placed warning signs around their work and then, I assumed, scuttled away chortling. The shops we passed sold nothing but deep-fried food. Ken's face was still thunderous, and my appetite had gone.

Eventually, on the outskirts of town, we saw an open coffee shop that advertised sandwiches. Ken parked while I went into the gloomy interior. The shop was deserted except for a severe-looking woman in her early fifties who was fiddling with some bits of paper behind the counter. When I asked whether she could make some sandwiches, she looked at me as if I was about to stab her in the eye. 'Can't,' she said. 'We close at four.'

It was then about twenty to four. 'We don't want much,' I said. 'But if you don't have any bread left ...'

'Doesn't matter whether we do or not,' she snapped. 'We're closing soon.'

So it'll take you twenty minutes to make two sandwiches? 'But there's nothing else open,' I pleaded. 'We'd really appreciate ...'

Finally, and with very bad grace, she dragged some squares of soapy cheese out of the fridge and slapped them between four slices of buttered white bread. It crossed my mind to ask her to toast them, but I knew I would really be pushing my luck. So I thanked her, paid and walked back to the van. From habit I started making the incident into a funny story for Ken's benefit: more than anything just then I wanted to make him laugh. But one glance at his set face told me not to bother. I handed him his sandwich in silence.

We headed out on the road to Narromine, about forty kilometres away. The sun was low in the sky by now and deep shadows crawled across the road. 'We'll find a motel to stay in,' said Ken. 'Fine,' I said. It didn't seem the moment to point out that we had already passed several, all of which had NO VACANCIES signs out the front.

It was almost dark when we reached Narromine. The main street was wide and empty, with shutters on all the shops. Not a soul in sight. Give the place a few tumbleweeds and a horse or two and it would have been perfect for a Western, I thought. Ken took the road towards the Macquarie River, the route that led to Warren further north.

On the outskirts we passed a large, cheerful neon-lit sign proclaiming that this was the Peppercorn Motel. There was nothing to say it was full, and I greeted it with relief. After a whole day in the van next to a scowling, uncommunicative Ken, the idea of human company was very welcome. Maybe if Ken had a glass of wine in hand he might lose that hard, set expression, relax and be sociable.

But in the front office the manager, a short harried-looking man in his forties, shook his head. 'Sorry, we haven't got any rooms,' he said. 'Big gliding convention over Easter. Can't help you.' The next motel, he said, was about seventy kilometres away, in Warren.

It was now six in the evening and quite dark. 'Do you want to push on to Warren?' I asked Ken.

'No, I know a spot by the Macquarie River,' he said. 'We can stay there, in the van, overnight.'

We drove slowly along the bitumen for another kilometre or so; the street lights became fewer and further apart and the night closed around us. On the right I saw the dark gleam of water and soon our headlights picked out a wide, rough track. Ken turned the van slowly towards the river and we bumped down a track that widened into a stony clearing. He stopped the van and switched off the lights and the engine. Immediately we were engulfed by the dark and a silence so complete that it struck like a physical blow.

Ken climbed out and headed for some scrub dimly visible at the end of the clearing. I opened up the back of the van, put the lights on, and started pulling chops, potatoes and carrots out of the tiny fridge. It was too early for dinner and the Dubbo cheese sandwich was still heavy on my stomach, but at least this was something useful I could do. In the dim light

I watched Ken pull a large branch across the ground towards the van. He left it about three metres away then went back to collect more twigs. What was he doing that for? The night was cool but not really cold enough for a fire.

'Don't build a fire there, it's too close to the van,' I said snappishly. Ken either did not hear me or took no notice. He dropped the twigs onto the branch, lit them, came over to the van.

'Where's the bloody whisky?' he demanded.

'Oh for God's sake.' I walked over to the smoking wood, stamped on it to extinguish it properly and started to drag the large branch back outside the van's circle of light. It was heavy and I scratched my hands, which did not improve my temper. When I had finished, my back aching, I straightened up and looked at the sky. Above me was a glistening carpet of stars, clearer than I had ever seen, bright enough, as my eyes adjusted, to cast faint shadows on the ground. I watched a tail of light – a comet, satellite, plane? – carving a shining path across the sky.

'Ken, look!' I turned back towards the van.

He was crouching forward over the back of the van, his right arm outstretched. I thought he was reaching for the bottle of whisky and started to tell him that I had put it in the rack above. As I came closer I saw that he was slumped on his side, his eyes closed, and apparently snoring. Perhaps he had dozed off, tired after all that driving … But then I realised that this was not a snore at all, it was a long guttural rasp of breath, a deep and dreadful sound I had never heard in my life before.

Dear God.

I rushed over and pulled at him. 'Ken, Ken, wake up!' I shook him, frantically tried to do CPR, pounded his chest, shook him, tried to move his arms. He was unresponsive, inert. He was so tall, so big, I couldn't move him at all, I couldn't do anything. And that terrible sound went on and on.

Then it stopped.

I straightened up. Wisps of smoke drifted from the woodpile. Ken was still slumped forward, eyes closed. He looked strangely neat, almost demure. There were a couple of leaves in his hair. I brushed them away.

An ice-cold voice in my head said, *You need to get help. But tidy up first. Do it quickly.* Not looking at Ken, I replaced the food in the refrigerator, turned off the gas and the light, doused the woodpile with the water in the plastic jerry can.

Good. Now go back to Narromine. But I didn't want to leave Ken. What if he woke up and found me gone? I thought I should leave a note of some kind. But the writing materials were all packed away somewhere, and I didn't want to waste any more time. And so I grabbed a torch (*good thinking!*) and started up the stony slope.

As soon as I reached the bitumen I started to run towards town. After a minute or two I saw light on the road behind me, and heard the hum of an engine. I waved my torch frantically.

A small sedan pulled up beside me. Its driver, who as far as I could see was male, leaned over and wound down the window.

'You going into Narromine?' I asked. He nodded. 'Then can you please take me to the police station?'

There was a pause while he eyed me: a tall woman in jeans and a striped shirt, wild-eyed and red-faced. 'Why?' he asked suspiciously.

'I … I think my husband has just died,' I said. I still have no idea where those words came from.

His tone changed immediately. 'There's an ambulance station in town,' he said. 'I'll drop you there.'

I climbed into the front passenger seat. Silently, we headed into Narromine. The trip lasted less than five minutes. I was surprised to find how close to town we had been. *Please be open, ambulance station, please …*

Thank God, it was flooded with light. An ambulance was parked inside its bay, its back open, with two men standing close by. One was obviously counting supplies while the other, who had a clipboard and pen, was checking them off.

Neither was at all pleased to see me. 'Can I help you, love?' said the one with the pen. He was tall and dark-haired with an air of authority – evidently the senior of the two.

'Yes,' I said in my new calm, icy voice. 'I'm camped by the river with my husband and I think he's ... will you come back with me, please?'

The other man, who was fair and chubby-faced, shot a nervous glance at his colleague. 'We're just packing up,' he said.

'OK,' said the older man, with a sigh. 'Just give us a couple of minutes.'

To my frantic eyes they seemed to take an eternity; they looked as if they were working underwater. When they were ready I climbed into the front seat beside the driver, while the younger man crouched in the back. We headed out along the Warren road again. 'You nearly missed us,' said the driver. I noticed that he had a small razor scrape on his cheek, as if he had shaved hastily that morning. 'Another five minutes and we would have been on our way home.'

Maybe, I thought, Ken will be sitting up in the back of the van. Sipping his whisky and smoking a cigarette. And he'll say, 'Hello, possum! Where've you been?'

But everything was just as I had left it, with Ken still lying on his side. The smell of woodsmoke was overpowering.

The driver parked the ambulance; both men got out and bent over Ken. They seemed to take a long time.

Then the dark-haired man straightened up and walked over to me. He said quietly, 'I'm sorry, love.'

The local doctor, disturbed on his night off, glared at me like an angry terrier. 'Myocardial infarction,' he said matter-of-factly. 'Heart attack.'

'Would it have been … would he have been in pain?'

A shrug. 'More than likely.'

'I tried to do CPR …'

He looked at me pityingly. 'Nine times out of ten that doesn't work,' he said.

Maybe all day Ken had been feeling jagged pain in his chest or up his left arm to his jaw; maybe this explained his short temper and sullenness. I remembered his determination to drag that branch and make a fire, the effort that must have cost him. Crazy. But if he had been feeling bad, why the hell hadn't he said anything?

When I left the doctor I went to the local police station and called my family and Ken's. Kerry, after a long silence, said, 'I've been dreading this.' For the first time, I think, I realised just how Ken's children must have suffered because of his airy denials about his health. 'Come to us,' she said – a kindness I hadn't expected. We arranged that I would fly back to Sydney from Dubbo the following morning; the police would take me to the airport. They stored the van in the station garage.

At about ten that night I walked into the dining room of the Peppercorn Motel. I was grubby, scratched, still reeking of smoke. I was also completely dry-eyed. The manager offered his condolences and said that a camp bed had been made up for me in the kitchen annexe. No, I didn't have to pay, this was on the house. When I thanked him, for I was genuinely grateful, he said hastily that the police had asked him to sort out my accommodation. He kept giving me nervous little glances and I wondered whether he was waiting for me to throw myself onto the porridge-coloured carpet and howl like a banshee. I felt like telling him he needn't have worried. I was managing beautifully.

He added apologetically that the kitchen was closed, but he could offer me some bread and a bit of cheese. My second cheese sandwich of the day. When asked what I would like to drink I said, 'Whisky, please.' A waiter brought me a glass, some water and a full bottle of Johnnie Walker. I ignored the water.

The dining room was still crowded, mostly with groups of men in jeans and windcheaters. They were probably having a final drink together and comparing notes about thermals and updraughts before bed. Sitting at a table in the corner were two couples who looked to be in their forties, evidently friends of the manager.

A large woman with a lot of blonded hair, red lipstick and cleavage was being the life of the party. 'Well, you know Bill,' she was saying while the others chuckled and nodded in agreement. The manager led me over to their table, which had the only spare seat in the room, introduced me and briefly explained what had happened. Their smiles faded as I sat down at the table with my cheese sandwich and bottle of Johnnie Walker.

'Hello,' I said. They told me their names, then stared silently into their drinks. They looked sombre and uncomfortable, and for the first time I understood the meaning of being *a skeleton at the feast.* I poured myself a huge neat whisky, the first of many.

The blonde woman finally took the initiative. 'Sorry to hear about your husband,' she said.

'Thanks,' I said.

'What did he die of?'

'Heart attack.'

'Oh, how old was he?'

'Fifty-seven.'

'That's very young,' said the oldest-looking of the men.

'How sad,' said the blonde woman sympathetically. 'But at least it wasn't bowel cancer.' She addressed everybody at the table. 'You know, you can get a kit to check.'

Pause.

'What did he do, your husband?'

'He was a writer.'

Politely raised eyebrows. 'What did he write?'

'Novels. One was called *Wake in Fright*. It was made into a movie a while ago.'

Is-that-so nods, without recognition.

'He also wrote books of funny short stories about the bush. One was called *The Killer Koala*.'

No reaction.

'He was on *The Ray Martin Show* a few weeks ago, telling stories from the books,' I said.

'I remember him, I saw that,' said the blonde woman quickly. 'A bloke with a beard, was that him? Wearing a Driza-Bone and an Akubra, and he was telling a story about a kangaroo that was drunk?'

'Yes, that's him,' I said.

She beamed. 'He was really funny, remember, Kev? Told this really good ... look, I couldn't stop laughing ...' She broke off and hastily rearranged her face into a more sombre expression.

'Such a shame this happened,' she said. 'Just when he was getting started.'

The annexe to the kitchen was a small room, harshly lit by a fluorescent tube, with cardboard boxes stacked around the walls. The smell of a hundred mixed grills stained the air. Below a window that would not open was a narrow, comfortless camp bed with sheets and a couple of blankets. I hadn't slept alone in a single bed for a long time.

But I knew I wouldn't sleep. I wasn't feeling tired, and even though I had drunk almost a whole bottle of neat whisky I was eerily sober. Sometime I would cry, I supposed, sometime the tears would come. But not now.

To the people I had met that night I was a youngish city woman, alone in a country town because she had just lost her husband. In my weirdly calm state, I thought the phrase had a certain Oscar Wildeish ring to it: *to lose one husband is unfortunate* … and so forth. Then I thought about the people I had met in the dining room. The blonde woman and her husband would be on their way home by now, and no doubt they would be saying to each other, 'That poor woman. Did you see how much whisky she drank?' I remembered the ambulance men. 'You're a brave girl,' the elder of the two had said. They were probably used to scraping twenty-year-olds off trees after car accidents. At least Ken and I had spared them that.

In that cold room I took off my jeans and top, cleaned my teeth at the sink in the kitchen, took off my bra, got into bed in my knickers. I hadn't worn anything to bed for many months. I lay on my back, staring into the darkness. *I love you, Jacqueline Kent, and I'm very grateful for your existence* … And still I could not cry.

PART 2

THE PAST IS UNPREDICTABLE

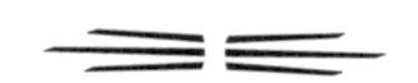

It is impossible to predict anything,
even the past.
RUSSIAN SAYING

EPITAPHS

Ken's death rated a small paragraph in several newspapers: death of a well-known popular writer, author of *Wake in Fright*, making no distinction between novel and movie. All stated that he had died of a heart attack in the outback as he was making a new journey around Australia – what an appropriate death for a writer of books about the bush! They all said that he had been alone.

In the first few weeks after I returned to Sydney, Ken was almost more vividly present than he had been when he was alive. This was true not only in the ten days or so I stayed with his children in James Street, but also when I briefly moved to the house of a friend, a place where Ken had never been. I would come into a room certain that I had just heard his voice, his deep rumbling laugh or smoker's cough, and several times out of the corner of my eye I saw a tall man with curly grey hair shuffling up the street ahead of me. I was desperate to hang on to him however I could. I used his words and phrases. If I was clumsy or obtuse I comforted myself by saying *poor mad creature* as he would have done; I declared that certain things made me *sad and cross*, as they did him. Using his words was like wearing the shirts and jumpers that still had traces of the smoky lemon scent of his body. I did that too. He sometimes came to me in dreams, and waking in the morning afterwards was hardest of all.

When I climbed into that camp bed in Narromine, I thought, *OK. I know what this feels like. I've been here before.* After Mum and Avril died, a kind of blank sadness had seeped into my bones, dragging but bearable; it has never entirely gone away, it will always be there. But the time after Ken's death was entirely different. It was devastating, violent. Suddenly, without warning, I would be swept under a wave of grief, like being held underwater by a huge hand. I literally couldn't breathe. It was like being waterboarded. When this happened, there was nothing I could do. It was awful. I don't know how I would have survived if these surges had happened all the time, and I thanked the gods that they did not.

However, mostly I continued to behave beautifully, following the dictates of that chilly, practical voice I had heard for the first time on the night Ken died. There was a perverse pride, I found, in not making a fuss. My reward was the relief I saw in people's faces that *thank God she isn't going to be difficult*, and I was praised for being *wonderful* and *strong*. I had yet to learn that, in Ruth Park's words, to be *wonderful* is to handle grief badly. But still nobody needed to know how scraped out, how hollowed, I felt most of the time. There was a thinness to everything, a shallowness that I think came from disbelief.

People were good, mostly. True, one or two expressed surprise that after a few weeks I still hadn't 'got over it'. After all, I hadn't known Ken very long, had I? But one old and dear woman friend whom I called late one evening in deep distress let me just talk to her for over an hour, without saying anything. I will always be grateful to her, and to those other friends who stood by when things were hard to bear. In that first week, I had a phone call from the senior ambulance man in Narromine, who was in Sydney visiting relatives. 'Just thought I'd call and see how you are,' he said gruffly. 'Hope you're OK. Look after yourself.' He was a very nice man.

'Wait until I'm dead and gone, love,' Ken used to say. 'They'll appreciate me then.' Sometimes he declared he would be quite happy to be shoved into a large green plastic bag and become landfill somewhere – after all, he wouldn't be around to see it happen. He would say such things when he thought the world was not too bad a place. When he was certain no good could come of anything, he would stare into his whisky and invent lines for his tombstone. I never knew how much of this was a theatrical game and how much was serious: now I think it was both. He must have known he would not live to be old; I later discovered he told Brian Davies that according to his calculations we would have ten years together. He made it a point of honour to tempt the Fates, those three ancient Greek guardians of human life. Maybe he thought that if he acknowledged the probability that he would die young, Atropos, the third and most feared of the Fates and the one who cut the thread of life, would stay her hand a little longer.

This is the epitaph he kept coming back to:

When I am dead
Let this be said
His sins were scarlet
But his books were read.

I don't know where Ken came across this – it's a quotation (slightly adapted) from the Anglo-French writer Hilaire Belloc. Perhaps he heard it as a young journalist discovering the work of Graham Greene,

Evelyn Waugh and their contemporaries. However, I have always thought those lines beautifully sum up the public Kenneth Cook: at once melancholy, self-deprecating and boastful.

They are the words on the stone slab that marks Ken's grave in Frenchs Forest lawn cemetery about fifteen kilometres north of the Sydney CBD. At least, I have been told they are; I have never actually seen them. I do not visit the grave of anyone I have loved. I can never see the point. Those who have gone are not to be found there.

As far as Ken's trustees in bankruptcy were concerned, nothing had changed. They started sending their threatening letters again. Some were addressed to me as 'the widow of Kenneth Cook deceased bankrupt', and I endured them for the next four years. Ken's children received similar letters. All carried the same message: *We know Kenneth Cook had a lot of money hidden away, and we intend to recover it. If you know what is good for you, and if you do not want to be prosecuted to the fullest extent of the law, you will tell us where this is hidden and allow us to get hold of it.*

Hard little beaks of worry kept pecking at me. What if the trustees discovered something we had genuinely known nothing about? Could we be prosecuted for perjury? Would I be able to keep the money I earned myself? And if Ken's children and I fought the trustees in court, how much, dear heaven, would it cost? Not surprisingly, all this drew Kerry, Megan, Paul, Anthony and me closer together. The weeks after Ken's death, in fact, were the high-water mark of our relationship. I felt, and I think they did too, that we were in one of those war movies where the good guys stand back to back in a circle, weapons drawn, while the enemy charges from all sides. *Contra mundum.* For the first time I was glad and grateful that we were united. I wanted us, the people Ken had loved most, to work together, to get rid of the trustees, to protect his legacy, to share our memories of him.

While I was staying at James Street immediately after Narromine I came to understand Ken's children better, to realise – as perhaps I should have done from the beginning – that their own needs and resentments were sometimes very different from those Ken had mentioned to me. At this time I also learned more about Ken's early life and career, and about his relationship with his parents, especially his father.

Kerry and her siblings said very little about their mother, of course, and I continued to wonder about Patricia. What sort of woman was she? And then, a couple of days before Ken's funeral, Kerry told me that Patricia had suggested we meet. This was not because of idle curiosity, sentimentality or fellow-feeling, I realised. She knew that on the day of the funeral people would be looking at us both, summing us up, noting how we reacted to each other. Each of us should at least know what the other looked like so we could behave appropriately and quash any unwelcome gossip. Considering that she might easily have considered me partly responsible for the maladroit divorce business, I thought her suggestion nicely combined the gracious and the pragmatic.

At the same time, I wondered what Ken would have thought about this particular twist in the plot – the whole idea of our meeting felt unreal in a made-up literary way. In a Greek tragedy or even a lugubrious Irish play, Patricia and I would have been robed in black, surrounded by a keening chorus, exchanging tokens of mutual sorrow. Instead one evening I found myself knocking politely on the front door of a neat apartment not far from the waterfront in Manly.

It was opened by a slight woman with carefully cut short dark hair, and neatly dressed in jeans and a white shirt. She looked smaller than the woman I had seen on the seafront that day, shorter than the length of her stride had suggested, and much younger than Ken, though I knew there were only a couple of years between them. I wondered whether she was as nervous and curious about meeting me as I was about her, but her large dark eyes, so like those of her daughter and granddaughter, gave nothing away. In a slow and rather drawling voice she said, 'Hello. Ken and I had our moments, but they are nothing to do with you. I'm very sorry about what's happened.'

The living room was small and sparsely furnished, without family photographs (Ken had never displayed any either). The room had a temporary feel, though not in quite the same way as Ken's living room in James Street. Ken's belongings had been pulled together in a student-housing style; Patricia's living room appeared to be the domain of a woman who had chosen carefully what she needed to have, nothing more.

Patricia made tea and we faced each other, straight-backed in armchairs like good children. We could have said a great deal to each other but I had no idea how or where to start and Patricia's reserve did not encourage confidences. Our great subject in common was hardly one we could explore, and so we carefully discussed the protocol of Ken's funeral without mentioning the reason for the service at all. Having been too blurred by grief to take much of an active role in the planning, I now learned that it was Patricia who had insisted on a full Catholic requiem mass and burial. 'We've asked Father O'Brien to run the proceedings,' she said. 'He's always been good at short sermons.' She gave me a swift ironic smile. I felt a brief stab of desolation. Patricia and her children, it seemed, were taking Ken back.

I thought what a strikingly attractive couple she and Ken must have made – he tall and commanding with black hair and green eyes, she slender and beautiful in a *quattrocento* style. I could readily believe a story Megan had told me, that when her parents met as members of an amateur dramatic society, they had practised duelling with imaginary swords up and down a city street. How exciting so much of their marriage must have been, too: Ken making his mark as a writer, helping to set up the TV production company he named after Patricia, the Butterfly Farm, parenthood, their involvement in protest and anti-Vietnam politics, theatre and folk music – and Patricia supporting his career and everything he did, every step of the way, until she no longer could.

Patricia and I spent an hour together. On parting we shook hands and formally wished each other well. As I walked up the Corso I reflected that here was a private woman, one who kept her own counsel, her enigmatic quality the antithesis of Ken's ebullient energy. At the funeral the following day Patricia and I smiled at each other and even hugged in full view of everyone there. We never met again.

Ken's death had left Margaret Gee, the publisher who had given him his new lease of literary life and final burst of success, with a marketing problem. The third volume of bush stories was ready to be published, except for the title story, 'Frill-Necked Frenzy'. It was at this point that I saw the Cook family factory in action. Ken's children met and discussed what should be done, and after they decided how the plot could go Megan, the daughter whose writing voice was probably closest to her father's, completed the story – and very well, too. I had no part in this, and it was only later that I realised what writing that story must have cost Megan, how difficult that whole arrangement must have been for them all. I edited the final manuscript, and that was hard enough.

With the stories typeset and printed and with a jokey, colourful cover, *Frill-Necked Frenzy* by Kenneth Cook was now ready to be released. But how could it be promoted, and by whom? Ken's previous publicity tour had been a bravura performance. How could anyone else compete with his level of professional showmanship? Margaret Gee decided it was best not even to try. In the end the publicity was mainly limited to local radio and newspaper interviews and features. However, some of the regional radio stations wanted someone from the family to do live interviews. None of Ken's children was willing to do it, and I said I would.

Looking back, I cannot believe I actually put myself forward for this. It was crazy. All I can say now is that I had convinced myself that this was what Ken would have wanted. *I can do this*, I told myself, *Ken died but I'm still alive, I have survived, I can survive anything. I'm a professional too. It is my duty to try and sell Ken's last book.* Armed with this grandiosity, I set forth.

The publicity campaign went about as well as might have been expected.

> ANNOUNCER ON COUNTRY RADIO STATION: *It's eleven minutes past two and you're with Bob* [or Len or Dave or Stevo]. *Now I want to tell you about something special coming your way a bit later on. We've got* [insert name of country and western singer, TV soap opera personality or local football star] *coming into the studio just after three. Yeah. I've been a fan of his* [always his] *since I was a young fella, can't wait to meet him. A real star.* [Sudden and obvious decrease of enthusiasm.] *But right now we're talking about books. Today it's, ah, a book of short stories,* Frill-Necked Frenzy *by Kenneth Cook. You might remember him, he was on the program a while ago, talking about his other book, to do with koalas it was. Very funny guy, told some great stories. Anyway, sadly Ken died of a heart attack a couple of months ago and we've got his widow, Jacqueline Kent, in the studio to talk about this latest book. How you going, Jacqueline?*

Margaret sent me to various places around Australia – it was still a time when commercial radio stations were often reluctant to conduct interviews by telephone – and sometimes I had hours, maybe whole days, alone in places I did not know. I came to dread the late afternoon about half-past five, the hour between dog and wolf, when the day is over and night has not yet begun. This can be the bleakest time of day when you are lonely and sad. Often I could not prevent the wolves from turning up.

When I had done most of the talking I was supposed to do, I visited Broken Hill. I had never been there, and it was *Wake in Fright* country – Ken had told me it had been one of the towns on which he based Bundanyabba. Broken Hill looked prosperous enough at first. The garishly lit pubs were doing the roaring trade that had surprised John Grant, though the two-up games had been replaced by poker machines that beeped and warbled. The saloon bar had clusters of women or soft-bellied men sharing a quiet talk and a pint or two, not sunbronzed, gnarled blokes demanding that city slickers have a drink with them. Broken Hill, it seemed, wasn't the place it had once been – not least because the mining industry, the lifeblood of the town, was undergoing a slump. On a bus trip around the area I saw deserted mines, with poppers and cranes creaking in the brisk, bitter wind. I also saw a large number of old cars, some apparently held together by red dust and string.

I also noticed something I thought was odd. The local paper carried many notices of houses for sale, but there seemed to be very few estate agents' signs on the winter-parched front lawns and fences, and the houses looked well cared for. When I asked why, I was told that most of them were vacant: their owners had moved away, seeking work elsewhere. But friends and neighbours were looking after the houses – mowing and watering lawns and making necessary minor repairs – to ensure they did not appear abandoned and therefore ripe for vandalism. Those cared-for houses expressed real mateship, real community caring – the opposite of the shallow, alcohol-fuelled bonhomie so scathingly depicted in *Wake in Fright*.

Wherever I went on that tour I carried a cassette tape of Chopin's piano music. Desolate and sleepless in Broken Hill, I played the 'Barcarolle', Op. 60, over and over again. Ever since, those first chords have carried me back to a bleak fluorescent-lit motel room. It is music of passion, then questioning and finally reassurance: of consolation, affirmation of tranquil beauty in the midst of darkness.

I carried that quiet comfort with me to Adelaide and Perth, where I next went, and then northeast again to Kalgoorlie. Because I have always loved travelling by train, I bought an overnight ticket on the Indian Pacific back to Adelaide. At about two in the morning the train stopped halfway across the Nullarbor at a siding named Cook. Largely because of the name I felt compelled to get out and have a look around. The light from the train picked out a scatter of small buildings, and the shadow of saltbush I knew stretched for hundreds of kilometres. I walked across a sandy hillock that concealed the track; it was utterly silent, the horizon was far, far away and the air was cold. I looked up. The stars blazed even more brightly than they had at Narromine. As I remembered that night and all that had followed, I waited for the familiar bleakness to descend, but it did not. Instead, I felt a tiny shift in the weight I was carrying, an almost imperceptible lightening of the spirit. Without conscious thought I stood up straighter, squared my shoulders and breathed deeply. For the first time I understood Ken's need to come out to places like this.

Then I realised that nothing but a railway line stood between me and the landscape. And I thought of the explorer John McDouall Stuart, stranded out here with fever. He had asked another member of his expedition to stay with him one night for, as he observed in his journal, *This is a very lonely place for a man to die in.* I looked up at the stars and shivered. And I turned and walked back across the sand, back to the train and the other passengers.

IN THE STONE HOUSE

The stone house was square and solid, with a graceful verandah facing the bay on the western side of Sydney Harbour. It was the tangible declaration by an ambitious Englishman that he had risen in the world, far from his working-class origins. Now, a hundred and thirty years after his death, the house was stranded among the rusty wheels and pulleys of the maritime industry that had created his success. I had been a guest in that house. I knew it as a sprawling and casual place, for music and argument and discussion, for pastime with good company. Similar houses in the area were eagerly being redecorated to look as they might have done when they were new, with carefully chosen furniture and carpets and lamps and ornaments. But the owners of the stone house, children of the 1960s, preferred their own family bits and pieces and cheap functional furniture.

This house was now my new temporary home. For nearly a year after Ken's death I was an urban gypsy, a housesitter, looking after the homes of friends while they were overseas. I couldn't bring myself to move back to the Queenscliff apartment – that had been Ken's and my place and I couldn't bear the thought of being there without him. Besides, it was still tenanted. So here I was, needing to move on in my life, and now I was moving house every few weeks. Sometimes the cosmos can be exasperatingly literal.

I was back doing the work I knew, and the vile machinery of Ken's bankruptcy had paused for a while. At last, I thought, I was beginning to come to terms with Ken's death and its aftermath. I was feeling better, I thought, at last doing what people said I should – get over it. Those devastating surges of feeling had gone; there were times when I felt positively cheerful. I was taking pleasure in life again. Ken's children and I had seen quite a lot of each other over several months, and we were getting on well. I felt as if I was coming to know them as the people they were, independent of their father. And so, full of optimism, one Sunday I invited them all over to lunch at the stone house: Kerry, her husband Chris and Sophie, Megan, Paul and Anthony. This was the first time I had seen them all together for some time, and I was looking forward to it.

We sat in the sunny garden on a warm, cloudy

afternoon and ate paella and salad and drank wine while the yachts glided past on the harbour. The year was drifting towards summer and the air was scented with jasmine. It was idyllic, beautiful. Yet I did not feel easy or comfortable, and for some time I did not realise quite why. Then I gradually noticed that without Ken to defer to or argue with, without his problems to acknowledge or rail against, his children were naturally talking about their own concerns. They chatted about careers and their mutual friends, they teased each other, recalled old jokes, laughed together. I suppose I could have been glad that the shadow had lifted for them too, at least temporarily, but I was unable to feel that. This was because they ignored me completely. I might as well not have been there.

After lunch, when they had all gone and I was collecting plates and glasses and scraping dishes, waves of desolation swept over me again. Ken's children and I were no longer as one in the way he would have wanted, and I felt bereft. As I washed up I asked myself, Had I imagined the closeness that had been so important to me over the past few months? Had it ever really existed, had I invented it out of my own need to try and keep their father beside me?

I told myself I had to face facts. My relationship had been with Ken, not with his children, and that had never really changed. My need to keep close to Ken's family for his sake had led me to mistake an alliance of circumstance and convenience for friendship. For their part, there was no reason why we should all be friends just because we had all loved their father. That lunch had told me so very clearly. But if I lost Ken's children, if we were estranged, I had also lost – really lost – him, and I was desperate that this should not happen. I knew I had to make some signposts for myself.

I started keeping a diary in the form of letters to Ken. I poured out everything that had happened since his death, everything I felt about him, about us, his family, the future. Doing so, writing for my eyes alone, felt odd at first, like dancing by myself, but it steadied me. I felt less like a small, frightened crab without a shell. And the act of writing, the sheer need to put down words in an orderly way, also helped me think clearly about the future.

It was in that stone house that one morning I woke from a dream knowing two things: Ken had been there, beside me – and he told me that he had to go. I heard him say so, as clearly as if I had heard his voice. And I had said goodbye to him, and I did not feel sad, because the last words he said to me were: *As long as you have me as part of your suit of armour, you'll be all right.*

Yes, but he wasn't there. And I still had to decide how to go on. I had to do something about my own interests, which were not the same as those of Ken's children. First of all, I needed someone to represent me in dealing with Ken's trustees. And so, apprehensively, I employed a lawyer recommended by a friend. It was a good decision. He was practical and effective, and having him on board clarified my thinking further.

Then came a body blow. In a casual conversation with Kerry, I discovered that Ken's children had sold The Company's last remaining asset – the Queenscliff apartment. Ken's and my home. They hadn't told me they even intended to do such a thing. I wished they had discussed this, and I still do. We could certainly have come to some arrangement. Once I started work again, I had intended to continue with the mortgage. But the Cook children had heavy legal expenses, the apartment could be sold, and I believe they wanted to avoid a difficult conversation with me. They were quite within their legal rights to sell the place: they were the effective representatives of The Company, whereas I was simply a director. I didn't make a fuss about the sale – what was the point? The thing was done, I had to get on with the rest of my life. At least this was a clean break, though I didn't consider this a source of consolation at the time. However, the business over the apartment effectively marked the end of my contact with Ken's children.

My own solicitor's fees were finally paid – I assumed

from the proceeds of Queenscliff – so though I had no home I wasn't seriously out of pocket, whatever the rights and wrongs of the sale. I had work I could still do. And I didn't have a dependent child, thank God. How complicated *that* would have been. There was still room for optimism, for making my own decisions – and to think about what Ken had meant to me. Dad, of all people, gave the pithiest summary of the situation: 'Well, beaut, he did you a certain amount of good and he didn't do you much harm.'

I thought of going away for a while, perhaps to France or Spain. It would be fun, I thought, to have more of those small satisfying adventures that travel bestows. Sure, I had hardly any money, but so what? I'd travelled on the cheap before. But I realised that I was no longer a freewheeling twentysomething looking for new experiences. I was a thirty-nine-year-old widow. Besides, why visit favourite places again when I could not turn to the person I most wanted to be with and say, *Look at this, isn't it wonderful?* Better, I thought, to stay at home among familiar places and faces I knew. Being by myself was all right. But now I knew there was all the difference in the world between living alone by choice and by circumstance. I had people I wanted to spend time with, to go to movies and restaurants with, to visit. What I no longer had, of course, was somebody to do nothing with.

Learning to be alone again felt rather like having to acquire basic skills all over again: buying small quantities of food, and white wine instead of beer and whisky, for example, seemed odd. Cooking a meal just for myself did too. Perhaps not surprisingly, I lost a lot of weight very quickly. And yet at the same time I rediscovered small pleasures. One day I went for a walk by the harbour with a friend and his independent border collie. The dog slipped her lead and took off across an oval and the owner and I raced after her. I was almost shocked at the sheer physical pleasure of running across grass – not having to slow my pace or wait for Ken, as I had had to do so often. I came back to the music I liked, went to concerts again, remembered old favourites and discovered new pianists and violinists and orchestras. I embarked on piano lessons for the first time since school and even took up jazz singing (which, I discovered, can be like telling your dreams: more fun to do than to listen to). I read thrillers, I discovered new writers, Australian and otherwise. And I could still laugh. After some months, when I described Ken's death to an Australian writer whose family came from Italy, she looked at me sympathetically and said, 'Oh, that's so sad.' I said yes, it was, but we hadn't been on the Gibb River Road miles from anywhere, and I hadn't been pregnant and about to give birth in the bush when he died, and we hadn't run out of food or water ... She said, 'Are you sure you're not Italian?' Sometimes I thought, *Come back, Ken, so I can show you how well I am doing without you.*

Engulfed as I had been in Ken and his world, I had been in danger of forgetting something very important: Dr Samuel Johnson's dictum that one must keep one's friendships in constant repair. Now, uncertainly at first, for I had neglected some long-standing friends for what seemed like a long time, I made connections again, and people were kind enough to welcome me back.

An important source of solace was a woman who lived within walking distance of the stone house, whom I sometimes visited after dinner. She would leave her very young baby with her husband for a while and we walked through the hushed, jasmine-scented darkness to a bare old pub to join the old men who were frowning into their beers and arguing over long-ago union disputes. We talked about books and writing and I felt something in me stretching, as it had not done for some time. My meetings with this friend were important to me. They reaffirmed friendship, but they also gave me something else: reassurance that the world I had known before Ken was still there, and that I was still part of it.

AFTERWORD

It's now more than thirty years since Kenneth Cook died. In that time, much has changed. The bedizen-worthy jewellery Ken had taken such pride in giving me disappeared in a house robbery and the theft of a bag from a train on the way to the Blue Mountains – even my wedding ring went. The apartment building in Queenscliff where Ken and I lived was torn down, to be replaced by a putty-coloured block of expensive town houses. About all I now have from our time together, in a tangible sense, are the Ho Chi Minh telegram and the exercise book.

There are so many things I wish I knew about Ken. First of all, of course, I wish I had been able to convince him to look after his physical health better. It might have been too late for that to make any difference by the time I met him, but I still wish I had known how to do that. I wish we had been able to talk properly about his damaged heart, the possibility that the time bomb ticking away inside him could explode at any time. Nobody could ask him about that. Difficult though it would have been for him to talk about all this, hard though it would have been for me to hear it, I wish he had taken me into his confidence. But that was not his way.

I wish I had known how to ask him more about himself, about the events and people that shaped him, that mattered to him, how he saw himself as a man and a writer. What had his religion meant to him, how had his attitudes changed since he embraced Catholicism so wholeheartedly as a young man? Like so many other Australian Catholics, he had rejected the Church's position on the Vietnam War, though he supported it on abortion. What other issues were important to him?

I wish he had written more novels. His son Anthony said to me once that he thought his father had been lazy, not challenging himself as a writer. There may be something in that; words always came so easily to him, he knew how to write the books he did – and evidently felt no need to stretch himself. I think he wore his talent too lightly, he didn't work it. It used to worry me that he spent so much time not writing, but that was his choice. It could also be that as his health declined he didn't have the stamina to keep writing novels – there were other things to do. However, I think the epitaph he chose for his gravestone was significant: he wanted to be remembered as Kenneth Cook the writer.

This is the story of Kenneth Cook and me – its beginnings, the course it ran and what happened afterwards. It has never been intended as a biography or autobiography, though of course it has elements of both. It's not a book of literary criticism either; Ken's body of work, though large, contains a great deal of journeyman writing. It's cheering that his best work is being re-evaluated. *Wake in Fright*, back in print, has found a new audience, and so did the miniseries on commercial television a couple of years ago. Some of his other novels are being republished. And the movie version of *Wake in Fright*, which follows the action of the novel very closely, is widely acknowledged as a classic of Australian cinema.

I met Ken when he had just emerged from a bad patch. We didn't have long together – not nearly long enough – but I want to salute the kind of person, in this case a man, who no longer seems to exist in the relatively pinched, cautious literary world of today. He was someone who spent his time and talent lavishly, who lived intensely, hard and wild: one who refused to measure out his life with coffee spoons. I also want to tip the hat to another time, when there were more enthusiasts and entrepreneurs in the book publishing industry than marketing managers, when a deal might be signed on a handshake, when a book might be published because someone, usually an editor, argued passionately in its favour, when relationships – between editor and author, author and publisher – were acknowledged as the lifeblood of the industry, rather than the decisions of bean counters. In our very different ways, Ken Cook and I were part of this rather lunatic, passionate industry – one that also deserves to be celebrated.

Memory is all very well, but it's not enough. Ken would have been amused to learn the first place I went in order to find him for this book: the National Library of Australia. I've always enjoyed going there. I like the unpretentious exterior – a cross between a Greek temple and a lunchbox – and the workmanlike reading room. It's a library that never weighs you down with a sense of literary duty or a feeling of inadequacy in the face of the rich and wonderful material it contains. Melbourne's La Trobe Library or Sydney's Mitchell – or the New York Public Library or the British Library, come to that – always make me wilt a little, seeming to say that in the presence of all this history and knowledge readers had better find something useful or interesting, with a masterpiece to follow, or they will be wasting posterity's time. The National Library has always seemed to say to me: *Come on in, see what you can find here. Feel free.*

I came across an interview Ken had recorded in the 1970s as part of the National Library's oral history project. For some people photographs most clearly and immediately bring a person back; for me voices do this. This may be a legacy of lifelong poor eyesight or perhaps my early experience in radio, but the sound of someone speaking, their characteristic accent, hesitations, phrases, pauses, emphases – all these things are to me more vital, more intimate and alive, than any image.

Listening to Ken's voice again, that deep voice with its rounded tones and old-style radio-play quality, was disconcerting: he sounded so immediate, so present. I was amused to notice how carefully he was enunciating his words, as he sometimes did for difficult phone calls or recording, the vocal equivalent of sitting up straight, shoulders back. And I thought it was characteristic that all he said about *Wake in Fright* was: 'I don't know what the damn book's about. It was something I had to do.'

As I packed up and returned the CDs to the librarian I thought how comforting it had been to hear Ken again, to be in his warm and companionable presence, even in this limited way. Then a thought struck me: Ken had made that recording in 1972. His children were now older than he had been then. And because of the things that had happened to him after he made that recording, some of which he had brought on himself, the cheerful man in his early forties whom

I had just heard was not quite the same man I met some years later. But then I was not quite the woman he had known either.

Ten years after Ken died, I found love again. But let my partner be an hour late home without explanation, let him have more than a bad cold, and I panic – I can't get away from the thought that time and fate might have engineered another catastrophe. That's a legacy of Ken too.

As I say, I wish I had more tangible mementoes of my life with Ken. But there are, of course, less material keepsakes. Like the only formal joke I ever heard Ken tell, and one I still think is funny. It's about a man who sees his friend hand in flipper with a penguin. 'What shall I do with this penguin?' asks the friend. The man says, 'Take him to the zoo.' The next day the man sees his friend again, still with the penguin. 'I thought I told you to take him to the zoo,' says the man. 'We went to the zoo yesterday,' says his friend. 'Today we're going to the movies.'

There are the phrases, too, of course. *Come and talk to me*, Ken would say, and now I say it myself. Being *sad and cross*, *causing deathless offence*, recommending chastisement *with whips and scorpions*, observing that someone is *drunk as an owl*: all are part of my vocabulary. And what I also carry now, and always will, is the knowledge that he loved me and I loved him, and that our brief time together, whatever its difficulties, was also rich and precious.

Some months after Ken died a newspaper journalist wrote, 'Farewell, Kenneth, and thanks for the stories.' He would have liked that.

He told me that once he was driving somewhere with Megan, aged about ten, in the back seat. She had started singing a song by the Bee Gees:

It's only words
And words are all I have
To take your heart away …

Those words affected him so strongly, he said, that he had to pull over and bring the car to a stop.

APPENDIX 1

AUSTRALIAN DICTIONARY OF BIOGRAPHY ENTRY

Cook, Kenneth Bernard (1929–1987)
by Jacqueline Kent

Kenneth Bernard Cook, novelist and film-maker, was born on 5 May 1929 at Lakemba, Sydney, and named Bert Kenneth, third and youngest child of Herbert Warner Cook, inspector for a time-payment firm, and his wife Lily May, née Soole, both born in New South Wales. His father left the family soon after. Kenneth attended Fort Street Boys' High School, then became a cadet on the *Richmond River Express* at Casino while also writing essays, stories and plays. He worked as a journalist in country towns and in Sydney for some years. Acting with the Genesian Theatre company in Sydney, he met a librarian and researcher, Irene Patricia Hickie, whom he married on 17 March 1951 at St Canice's Catholic Church, Elizabeth Bay.

In 1952–54 Cook worked for the Australian Broadcasting Commission, at Broken Hill – a town he loathed – and then at Rockhampton, Queensland. There he wrote a novel which, initially accepted, was later considered libellous and pulped. After six months in Brisbane, he returned to Sydney in November 1954. He resigned from the ABC in 1961 and that year published his best-known novel, *Wake in Fright*, which drew on his experience in Broken Hill. The novels *Chain of Darkness* (1962) and *Stormalong* (1963) followed; royalties together with successful real-estate speculation enabled him to take his family overseas for an extended holiday, described in *Blood Red Roses* (1963). Back in Australia, he, Philip Hickie and John Crew set up Patrician Films Pty Ltd to make television films, mainly for children.

Cook stood for Federal parliament twice, unsuccessfully: in 1966 for the seat of Parramatta on behalf of the Liberal Reform Group on an anti-conscription ticket, and in 1969 for Bennelong as an Australia Party candidate. A Catholic of liberal views, he opposed the Church's stand on the Vietnam War. He expressed his passionate opposition to the war in the novel *The Wine of God's Anger* (1968), and – couched as government oppression at Eureka – in the musical play *Stockade*, first performed in 1971. *Stockade* and *Wake in Fright* were released as films that year.

Continuing to write with the aid of Commonwealth literary grants, Cook published many novels including *Tuna* (1967) and *Pig* (1980), two of his best books. He separated from Patricia; they were later divorced. The butterfly farm that he had established on the Hawkesbury River failed; in 1983 he was declared bankrupt after personally guaranteeing a film project. Ill and depressed, he wrote *The Killer Koala* (1986), the first of three collections of comic bush stories, contrasting the heroic image of the Australian bush and the stark reality: the amusing obverse of *Wake in Fright*. Sales of 30,000 copies helped to restore his confidence, as did his marriage to Jacqueline Frances Kent, a writer and editor, on 5 January 1987 in a civil ceremony at St Leonards, Sydney.

Survived by his wife and the two daughters and two sons of his first marriage, Cook died of myocardial infarction on 18 April 1987 at Narromine. He was buried in Frenchs Forest lawn cemetery.

A consummate professional, he wrote novels, plays, songs, screenplays, and radio and television scripts. At heart he was a storyteller, and he knew how to treat serious, even tragic, themes with compassion and a light touch. Probably because of his popular success, he was an underrated Australian writer.

APPENDIX 2

'MY WORKS': BOOKS BY KENNETH COOK

Wake in Fright, 1961
Chain of Darkness, 1962
Stormalong, 1963
Wanted Dead, 1963 (under pseudonym Alan Hale)
The Take, 1963 (under pseudonym John Duffy)
Vantage to the Gale, 1963 (under pseudonym Alan Hale)
Blood Red Roses, 1963
Tuna, 1967
The Wine of God's Anger, 1968
Piper in the Market-Place, 1971
Bloodhouse, 1974
Eliza Fraser, 1976
The Man Underground, 1977
Play Little Victims, 1978
Pig, 1980
The Judas Fish, 1983
The Film-Makers (with Kerry Cook), 1983

The Killer Koala, 1986
Wombat Revenge, 1987
Frill-Necked Frenzy, 1987
Life on the Edge: Bloodhouse, Tuna, Pig, 1988
Fear Is the Rider, 2016

CAPTIONS

Page 19 Ken's favourite photograph of me, taken by him soon after we met.

Page 76 Ken's mother, Lily; Ken, from a photograph taken in Eden, New South Wales, late in 1986.

Page 89 The wedding of Norma Gardner and Lance Kent, St Mark's Darling Point, June 1946.

Page 91 Happy families: taken at our house in Normanhurst, Sydney, in about 1956.

Page 93 Me, Mum, Mardi and Avril at Mardi's graduation, University of Sydney, May 1972, photo taken by Dad. I left for London in October of that year.

Page 129 Ken in full flight.

Page 160 Ken, late at night in our Manly apartment.

Page 169 On the road, Eden, New South Wales.

Page 176 *Top:* 6 January 1987, in the garden of the Stationmaster's Cottage, St Leonards. *Bottom:* Dad, me, Ken and Mardi after the ceremony.

Page 177 In our wedding garb.

Page 179 'Come here, woman, and marry me.'

Page 231 Together, south coast of New South Wales, late 1986.

ENDNOTES

Page 2 *they were not rats but ferrets*
I think he was referring to the weekly newspaper *The National Times* (1971–86), which had as its motto 'lean and nosy like a ferret' and featured lugubrious creatures as dinkuses.

Page 5 *because he was he, because I was I*
In his famous essay 'On Friendship' Michel de Montaigne (1533–1592) wrote about his dear friend Étienne de la Boétie, describing their relationship in these words: 'If you press me to say why I loved him, I can say no more than because he was he, because I was I.' (Michel de Montaigne, *Essays*, translated with an introduction by J. M. Cohen, Penguin Books, London, 1993, p. 97.)

Page 35 *he told me, and I said I would.*
Ken preferred *God Knows* (Pan Macmillan Australia, Sydney, 1984) to *Catch-22*. I can't quite agree, but it is very nearly as hilarious, with some good Jewish jokes.

Page 36 *named after his wife Patricia*
Patrician Films was set up by Ken's brother-in-law Philip Hickie in 1964, and Ken wrote and directed children's films for it, which they sold to the ABC. The company specialised in short films, including series *Lens on Lilliput* and *Lens on Life under the Sea*. Such films were needed to fill the ten minutes left for ads in imported hour-long programs.

Page 37 *And it's only money.*
The Butterfly Farm, set up in 1972 by a consortium of Ken, his friends and businessmen, was originally a caravan park with water-skiing facilities close to the Hawkesbury River at Wilberforce, near Windsor, on the northwestern outskirts of Sydney. About fifty acres in extent, the land had a large house on a nearby slope, which they decided to make into a museum for a collection of butterflies and other insects. The Butterfly Farm cost almost $400,000 to set up – an enormous amount at the time (*The Sydney Morning Herald,* 26 November 1972, p. 17). According to those who now run the farm,

the hundred-year floods made a bad financial situation worse.

Page 41 *nothing more to do with snakes after that.* Kenneth Cook, 'Vic the Snake Man', *The Killer Koala*, Tortoiseshell Press, Sydney, 1986, p. 37. Early in 2011 while I was listening on iPod to the Chicago Public Radio program *This American Life*, I was astonished to hear a man with an Australian accent telling exactly the same story. He turned out to be Luke Davies, the son of Ken's great friend Brian Davies, who was involved with the Butterfly Farm. Luke is a poet, arts journalist and author of the enormously successful novel *Candy*, and winner of an Oscar for best adapted screenplay for the movie *Lion* in 2017. He was, in fact, the young boy who was sent running for that pint of milk. Luke later told me that his first published short story was a fictionalised version of the events, called 'Venom', and that it appeared in *Smashed*, an anthology of Australian drinking stories edited by Matt Condon and published by Random House Australia in 1996. (Email communication 13 December 2011)

Page 49 *the only Australian novel about the Vietnam War.* This was true until the publication of Christopher Koch's Miles Franklin Award-winning novel *Highways to a War* (William Heinemann Australia, Port Melbourne, 1995).

Page 53 *He wrote up the story of the court case, with its principals heavily disguised*
Ken never said so, but it's probable that the 'character' he meant was Rex Pilbeam, mayor of Rockhampton in the 1950s when Ken had been stationed there. See www.themorningbulletin.com.au/news/60th-anniversary-former-mayor-shot-by-his-lover/1898766/

Page 90 *as described in his memoir*
Robert Drewe, *The Shark Net*, Penguin Books Australia, Melbourne, 2000.

Page 101 *to destroy him and his country.*
I was half expecting Ken to have an ASIO file as a result of this – other writers acquired them with, one would imagine, much less cause – but he never did. More than likely this was a source of disappointment to him, as was his often-expressed chagrin at his failure to acquire a criminal record.

Page 108 *many of which were never made.*
Division 10BA (1981) of the *Income Tax Assessment Act 1936* was a rort of enormous proportions. This was gradually whittled away throughout the 1980s as the government realised how much tax revenue they were losing. However by 1989, 10BA was still a flat 100 per cent write-off.

Page 121 *Military Cross during the war.*
Details of the Balikpapan landing and my father's Military Cross can be found in A. L. Graeme-Evans, *Of Storms and Rainbows: The Story of the Men of the 2/12 Battalion AIF*, vol. 2, March 1942 – January 1946, 12th Battalion Association, New Town, Tasmania, 1991, p. 423 foll., and at the Australian War Memorial website www.awm.gov.au/collection/U56055

Page 139 *for his own contemporaries.*
Ken also considered that Australian literature was becoming the creature of the academy. In the 1970s and 1980s Australian literature courses began to be offered in Australian universities, though there was only one professor of Australian literature – at the University of Sydney – until 1996. Hardly an onslaught.

Page 139 *But he didn't praise any of the others.*
One writer Ken would certainly have liked and admired is Peter Temple, especially for his novel *The Broken Shore* (2005). Temple wrote an introduction to the Text paperback version of *Wake in Fright* (Text Publishing, Melbourne, 2013).

Page 156 *popular with amateur theatre and music groups.*
While we were together Ken received several requests for permission to have *Stockade* performed. The play

came out of the early-1970s vogue for musical plays based on events or characters in Australian history. Probably the best known example is *The Legend of King O'Malley* (1970) by Michael Boddy and Bob Ellis, originally directed by John Bell. *Stockade* was an episodic play dramatising the main historical events, portraying Eureka Stockade's leader Peter Lalor as a romantic rebel battling against evil and powerful government forces. The play explores the need for violent confrontation and resistance and there were, of course, parallels with opposition to the Vietnam War. Music for the play, and the film subsequently made from it, came from traditional sources. Ken and Patricia Cook wrote new lyrics. The text was later published by Penguin Books (Ringwood, Victoria, 1975).

Page 174 *thinking it was rather soppy.*
Christina Rossetti (1833–1894) was an English poet, probably best known today for her poems 'When I Am Dead, My Dearest' and 'Goblin Market'.

Page 204 *Anglo-French writer Hilaire Belloc.*
The actual quotation is: 'When I am dead/I hope it may be said:/His sins were scarlet/But his books were read.'

Page 209 *up and down a city street.*
Ken told me that he and Patricia met at the Genesian

Theatre, an amateur theatre group named after St Genesius, patron saint of actors, and formed in 1944 by the Sydney Catholic Youth Organisation.

Page 234 *an underrated Australian writer.*
Sources for this *Australian Dictionary of Biography* entry include *Westerly*, no. 3, 1977, p. 75; *The Bulletin*, 15 December 1973, p. 43; *The Sydney Morning Herald*, 27 June 1985, p. 1; *The Northern Herald* supplement, 21 April 1987, p. 4; J. Kent, 'Jacqueline Kent Remembers Kenneth Cook', *Australian Author*, July 1987, p. 3; H. de Berg, interview with Kenneth Cook (transcript, 1972, National Library of Australia); personal knowledge.

ACKNOWLEDGEMENTS

I owe a great debt to a number of people for their help in getting this book to publication.

First of all I thank Suzanne Falkiner, present for much of this story, for her engagement with the manuscript and her invaluable comments. I thank also my agent, Jane Novak, who galvanised me into action when the manuscript was at a critical stage and provided practical help; and Ben Ball, Meredith Rose, Rhyll McMaster and Mary Cunnane for close and insightful reading of early drafts. Mardi Kent checked certain family details, including our father's war record, and I thank her above all for her forbearance. Brian Davies filled in some important gaps in my knowledge of Kenneth Cook's life. Luke Davies supplied information about Vic the Snake Man and other aspects of life at the Butterfly Farm.

I am also grateful to Alexandra Payne at the

University of Queensland Press for her enthusiasm about the book: working with her, Cathy Vallance and the others on the staff of UQP has been one of the most pleasant experiences in my writing life. Thanks also to the staff of the Butterfly Farm at Wilberforce, New South Wales; librarians at the National Library of Australia, Canberra, and the Mitchell Library, Sydney; and the Glebe Readers, especially Joy Storie. Last but certainly not least, I thank John Tuchin for help and support of many kinds.